Della

Please Enjoy

Elaine Hegwood Bowen

Old School Adventures from
ENGLEWOOD—
SOUTH SIDE OF CHICAGO

ELAINE HEGWOOD BOWEN

ISBN: 978-1-4834-1453-9 (sc)
ISBN: 978-1-4834-1452-2 (e)

Library of Congress Control Number: 2014912300

Lulu Publishing Services rev. date: 07/29/2014

This book is dedicated to the memory of my father, Randolph Hegwood Sr., who was affectionately called "The Warden" by me and my siblings. I want to thank my mother, Pinkie, for all her sacrifices to make sure that we were brought up as well-mannered, respectable children who grew into wholesome adults. I want to thank my siblings, Randy, Audrey, Phyllis, Olivia, R.L. and Gloria Jean, who helped me remember experiences that I had forgotten. I also want to thank those friends and extended family members who helped make up those experiences. A special thanks to Olivia for countless hours of spiritual encouragement and editing assistance. I thank my daughter, Cristalle Elaine, who not only made me proud when she earned her Chemistry degree from the University of Illinois at Urbana-Champaign, but who continues to make me most proud when she selflessly works with youth throughout Chicago and the nation with Rhymeschool.

I thank God for my talents and health.

Prayers and encouragement to families all over who have been affected by violence. This, too, shall pass!!

Prologue

I offer this book as a story, not of nihilism and despair, but one of promise about the coming of age of a little girl and her siblings in the Englewood community on the South Side of Chicago. I grew up in a big, white house in that community. And since we now have had an official black family—the Obamas—in the esteemed big, White House, I figured this book would serve as a nice complement to what is known about First Lady Michelle Obama's childhood and mine. Just like the First Lady, I am also a "little black girl from the South Side of Chicago."

Much has been written about the Englewood area within the past few years. In fact, she even visited Harper High School, which is located in Englewood, to speak with students there who had been overwhelmed with just trying to survive poverty and the daily violence. I was thrilled when the First Lady visited Harper because I felt that when Pres. Barack Obama spoke at Hyde Park Academy, in the beginning of 2013, he should have very well been at Harper. Previously, Harper and its violent environment had been profiled on National Public Radio. But Hyde Park Academy is located in Hyde Park, the area where the Obamas lived before they went to the White House, and I can understand that connection.

Reporter Don Terry covered the crime in Englewood in a *New York Times* article that published February 4, 2012, and was titled "In South Side neighborhood, violence still hard to take." The story detailed one family's struggle to keep their children safe in an area besieged by crime and gang activity. The story discussed a shooting on the previous January 15th and also a shooting at a local chicken restaurant during that previous Christmas season. "There's no escape," the mother was quoted in the article as saying. "Living in Englewood, I feel like I'm robbing my children of their childhood."

Other news outlets have carried news not only about the crime in Englewood, but on the South Side and other parts of Chicago, as well, as evidenced by the following *Chicago Sun-Times* article dated July 8, 2013.

Killing Fields – 38 shootings during four-day holiday weekend leave 10 dead, 55 wounded.

This year's Independence Day celebration, for many Chicagoans a four-day respite in the land of the free, was for others an ordeal in a killing field. Violence tore through parts of the city from Wednesday night to Sunday night. Police and community sources said the bloodshed was driven by gang warfare, good weather, easy access to guns and a reluctance of witnesses and the victims to identify the shooters.

The Chicago Sun-Times has counted 38 separate shooting incidents since 6 p.m. Wednesday. Ten men were killed and 55 other people, including two young boys, were wounded.

To date this year, there have been 202 homicides, down from 275 for the same time last year, according to Sun-Times data.

The carnage was tightly concentrated. Forty percent of the incidents occurred in and around two West Side neighborhoods — Austin and Garfield Park — roughly an 8.5-square-mile patch of a 228-square-mile city.

But when cable station HBO highlighted the issue with their special called *VICE* that illustrated the carnage, grit, and tragedy that were occurring in my birth home, I wanted to document that Englewood wasn't always that way. Englewood was previously known as a "step up" for blacks who were coming from other places in the city, such as my family. But times change, and crime seems to permeate the neighborhood, with many black youth taking their last breaths on the nasty, blood-stained streets of Englewood. But—if truth be told—one would have to admit that it's not just Englewood; crime is festering all across the city, and unemployed, poorly educated youth are easily caught up in the criminal elements associated with the drug trade, even though some experts will say that not all killings are due to drug trafficking; some are associated with territories and turf, especially with the dismantling of the celebrated projects and the disbursement of people into all areas on the South and West Sides. We can only hope that families are resurrected and restored, and children across the city and particularly Englewood can get back to living and enjoying life and only having to worry about securing an education—and not what route to take to school to dodge gang activity or bullets.

Until then, take a trip into my time capsule and share a few vignettes that will bring back joyful memories for some and hope for others that soon society as a whole will be more peaceful and forgiving. At the conclusion of most essays, my daughter, Psalm One, will offer poetry that connects my history and her personal insights.

One

Me [Elaine Hegwood Bowen, MSJ]

ello, I'm Elaine Hegwood Bowen. And no, I don't come from a long line of journalists. In fact, there are no journalists in my extended family. And some members, when they heard that I was studying journalism at Roosevelt University, would automatically proclaim, "You're going to be on television!" They also said, "I was at the bank the other day, but I didn't see you," when I told them years ago that I worked at First Chicago (Chase). Even though I was programming computers in the Resource Management Unit, they couldn't get past picturing me with the tellers on the first floor. I suppose that since they couldn't see me at the bank, they could at least anticipate seeing me on the evening news. No such luck! But good fortune and constant praying have helped me reach this point.

Of course, I'm no slacker or scrub. In fact, I consider myself an over-achiever. I was born on the South Side of Chicago in the mid-1950s and was graduated from Jones Commercial High School in the early 1970s. I had spent two years at Gage Park High School prior to that but transferred downtown to Jones after tiring of the almost daily race riots at Gage Park. My brother, Randy, experienced the same thing when he enrolled at the school a few years before me. "I had a hard time getting out of high school," he said, "But I did so much better when I graduated from DeVry Institute of Technology in the mid-1970s." He talked about the riots and white students throwing bricks at the buses during that time at Gage Park, while he rejoiced in transferring to another school.

"I used my cousin's address and enrolled at Calumet High School and finally graduated from Lindblom High School in the summer of 1971." Randy worked for twenty years as a technician with Western Electric, after having been recruited from DeVry. I guess it was good to be run out of segregated Gage Park. In hindsight, the only thing that I regret not doing at Gage Park, which I didn't have a chance to do at Jones, is learn how to swim. Since Gage Park was not quite used to Negroes, the swim teacher certainly didn't mind that most times we had some excuse or another to not participate in the swim lessons. I mean how many times can a young girl have a period? And when I did legitimately have a cycle, there was no way I was getting in the water—not while wearing that big, thick sanitary napkin. Oh, and let's not talk about a sistuh even taking a chance on getting her hair wet!

After graduation, I enrolled in Loop College (Harold Washington College). I did so with much reservation because I had vowed after Jones that I wouldn't attend college. You see, you could make a decent living with just a high school diploma back when I graduated high school; and I was more than qualified to perform office work. One of my closest friends who also went to Jones with me immediately enrolled in college and later became a Certified Public Accountant. I was happy with the classes that I took at Loop, which was one of the City Colleges of Chicago. It was at Loop that I was exposed to the joy and cultural significance of black literature. Under the instruction of Professor Flora Dejoie, I fell in love with James Baldwin, Richard Wright, Charles Waddell Chesnutt, the esteemed and indomitable Maya Angelou, Claude McKay, Ann Petry, Langston Hughes, Zora Neale Hurston, and other fine black writers and poets. Dejoie taught a Perspectives of Black Literature class, where my mind and heart opened to black writers to whom I had never been introduced. During her class, I learned about many who lived right here in Chicago. The first African American to win a Pulitzer Prize was Gwendolyn Brooks, who was a long-time resident and former poet laureate of Illinois. She won the Pulitzer for Poetry for her work *Annie Allen*. She had graduated from Englewood High School in 1934 and wrote poetry while living in a second-floor apartment at 623 E. Sixty-Third Street. Brooks is remembered in Chicago with lasting tributes that include the Gwendolyn Brooks College Prep Academy and the Gwendolyn Brooks Center for Black Literature and Creative Writing at Chicago State University.

Lorraine Hansberry also attended Englewood High School. Her *A Raisin in the Sun* was the first play by an African American woman to be produced on Broadway. Hansberry was from an upper-class family, and her father was a real estate agent on the South Side. Her play related the experiences of a black family as they integrated into an all-white neighborhood in Chicago. There was also Sterling Plumpp, Sam Greenlee, Margaret Burroughs, St. Clair Drake, and Margaret Walker, among others.

This class was phenomenal in that it taught me about literature in a way that I hadn't before imagined. But it was during an English course that I was taking in the First Chicago building that I met a young man who impressed me with movie passes to the Plitt Theaters. That particular theater chain isn't around anymore, but this experience just helped to further cultivate my love of films. To be able to enter the movies with a pre-paid ticket was so impressive, and it harkened me back to my teen years of going to the "show."

Movies have always been a source of entertainment for me, but they weren't as readily available as they are now on different media. Let's go back in time, when the movie *The Amazing Colossal Man* was playing at the neighborhood show and not at a colossal Cineplex complex; when *The Blob* was a red slimy thing and not *The Fat Boys* with Ralph Bellamy; when *The Sound of Music* was a musical starring Julie Andrews running through the meadows in full skirt and not *Sign 'O' the Times* with Prince and Sheila E. running around each other; when ... well, you get the picture.

During my early teen years, Sunday was the Sabbath—well it still is—and a day of going to Sunday School and morning service. And then there was the show. I was given "show fare" and extra money for refreshments. My siblings and I entered a particular show, the Empress, which was located on Sixty-Second Street and Halsted and was just one of a few movie theaters in the area. The theaters weren't the only businesses. There was also a Kresge's, Wieboldt's, Sears, Carr's Clothing Store, Walgreens, Frederick's of Hollywood, Paddor's Clothing, Raab Tailors (where all the cool bruthas would go to get tailor-made suits), among others. I recall walking to the Wieboldt's with two buddies who lived down the street. They would go there to exchange S&H green stamps for all kinds of small appliances or goods that were the result of their guardians shopping at the local grocery store and accumulating the stamps according to the amount of groceries that were purchased. In the late 1960s, this area was thriving with commerce and not just wig, sports wear, and dollar discount stores.

My siblings and I didn't need extra money for carfare on the "big green," the Chicago Transit Authority (CTA) bus, because we could easily walk to Halsted Street. Once at the show, we would pay the suggested price and then dash to the candy counter. Boston Baked Beans, Good 'N Fruity, licorice sticks, M&M's—a long way yet from nachos, gourmet coffee and VIP seating—and, of course, popcorn. It is hard to recall, reflecting back, if I had more fun eating popcorn or doing the dance called the Popcorn, introduced and made famous by the incomparable James Brown. Naturally, we were sharing among ourselves. We didn't eat much junk food or candy during the week, so to be able to get all sticky and greasy on the weekend was a welcome respite.

Even if the movie was bad, sitting in the poorly upholstered seats, but eating unlimited candy made all the difference in the world. It was quite the "buppie" thing to do. After several boxes of candy and numerous trips to the "baffrum" and, oh yeah, a movie or two we were on our way back home. Once there we may not have been able to recite a Bible verse, but we could surely report back on what Donald Duck or John Wayne was doing.

Back then, older folks went to the Englewood Theater, which would play movies for a more mature audience. So I was stuck with movies rated for general viewing, which at that time had more white cast members. But when the Blaxploitation era jumped off in the early 1970s, I was all ready, (well, sort of). Then we were going to the theaters downtown, namely the United Artists, Loop, McVickers, State and Lake, and the Oriental, among others, to see *Come Back Charleston Blue, Cotton Comes to Harlem, Claudine, Shaft, Superfly, Blacula, Cleopatra Jones*, etc. Going downtown meant dressing for the occasion. You couldn't go downtown looking like a wayward child with your hair flying every which way but loose. You had to be as fly and primped as the folks who jumped out at you from the movie screen. And you didn't go downtown broke! If you didn't have fare for the rapid transit (the Englewood-Howard elevated "EL" or the public train system that ran throughout the city, which included a station that was about three blocks from our home) and enough money to get in the movies and buy some snacks, then you weren't going anywhere. "You aren't going downtown to embarrass me," my mother would say. "If you don't have enough money for everything, then you may as well stay home. Can't be down there begging for money. You have to pay your own way."

North Side brings with the promise of not being the South Side. The ventures become adventures, and my eyes are wide. No window shopping allowed. Work for what you desire. Thriving business districts. Store credits. Reading my mother's book. More edits. I'm black and I'm very proud, yeah!

I said it! Walking up Sixty-Third Street, watching my back was a long way from seeing these thriving blacks. Still and all, the ghosts of classic times at the mall have shaped me from girl to woman. This neighborhood made me human. Made me jukin'!

-----Psalm One

The author as cute as a button in her mom's lap

Two

Early Family

M y mother could relate to paying her own way because she and my father worked hard to make a living and support our family. As with many Chicago families, my parents, Randolph and Pinkie, weren't born in Chicago. History tells us that Chicago is made up of folks from Alabama, Arkansas, Georgia, and Mississippi, to name a few states. My parents came from Shaw, Mississippi, to Chicago in the mid-1950s, as part of a migration of blacks to Chicago from down South. This decades-long exodus was called both the Great Migration and the Second Great Migration and began approximately in 1910 and lasted to around 1970. During this time, it's recorded that the city of Chicago attracted slightly more than 500,000 of the approximately seven million blacks who left the South for the streets up North that were paved with gold. Before 1916, blacks made up about 2 percent of Chicago's population; at the crest of the two migration periods—1970—we made up about 33 percent. A great deal of this movement can be attributed to one newspaper, the *Chicago Defender*, which was founded by Robert S. Abbott in 1905, with an initial investment of twenty-five cents. The paper was being left at posts throughout the nation by Pullman Porters, and the pages talked up a good game: that of putting down plows and putting up stakes in the North.

There were immense opportunities for blacks, in railroad yards, steel mills, packinghouses, and other industries, and wages were better than those that could be found down South. But because they were still black, workers didn't get as high a wage as their white counterparts. While not optimum, things were viewed as better, even though living arrangements may have been in cramped apartments or tenements. The sentiment is that anything was better than in the Southern states from where they had left, or I would say from where they had "escaped," since it is recorded that many blacks left their homelands in the dark of the night, afraid for their lives while driving or on the buses or trains.

Southern blacks also learned about the Northern towns from relatives who wrote about the "Promised Land" in letters that they sent back home. However, the black press, of which the *Chicago Defender* would eventually become a member, had begun years before. The first black newspaper was called the *Freedom's Journal* and was published in 1827 in New York City by Samuel Eli Cornish and John Brown Russwurm. It had the distinction of being the first newspaper owned, operated, edited, and published by black Americans. The first issue on March 16th of that year contained a five-point salutatory that was addressed "to our patrons" and signed "The Editors." The salutatory first held that the editors wanted to "offset any misrepresentations in publications originating from others who too long have spoken for us, often to the discredit to any person of colour." The *Journal* aspired to provide the Negro with his own forum. It said, in short, "We wish to plead our own cause." Other tenets spoke to "helping children become useful members of society through education; intensifying character development and the improvement of personal traits to raise the general level of conduct of free blacks; to vindicate our brethren, when oppressed, and to lay the case before the publick [sic], and finally to lead readers away from time-wasting, trivial publications and to enlarge their stock of useful knowledge."

The *Journal* continued publication for two years and then folded because Cornish wanted to devote his time to the ministry. Russwurm ran it alone for awhile but finally resigned, saying that the paper hadn't met success with its goals. He also attributed failure to widespread, continuing prejudice.

Other papers would be started across the country, and the Black press was full steam ahead, both literally and figuratively, in its struggle against racism. And once blacks settled here, the *Defender*, and later the *Chicago Crusader*, was brimming with news and information that helped them with all aspects of life in Chicago. The *Chicago Crusader* has been around since 1940, and it was founded by Balm L. Leavell and Joseph H. Jefferson. They were members of the Negro Labor Relations League, which put pressure on white companies to hire black workers for jobs, such as newspaper carriers, movie theater projectionists, and dairy truck drivers. Inherited by Dorothy R. Leavell, the widow of Balm Leavell, the *Crusader* is one of the oldest continuously running and successful black-owned newspapers in the nation. The paper is still known for taking up causes, such as unfair employment practices among local companies, in an effort to ensure that blacks can earn fair wages.

While the local newspapers were great sources of information for the new arrivals to Chicago, the Chicago Urban League is also noted for its participation in helping those new to the city find jobs. It is noted that urban leagues played the roles of advocates in many urban cities bustling with new residents who were used to sharecropping and doing other labor-intensive work in the towns in which they were born.

At a discussion about the Great Migration to Chicago and the success of Isabel Wilkerson's 2010 book *The Warmth of Other Suns: The Epic Story of America's Great Migration*, Adam Green, Associate Professor of American History at the University of Chicago, noted that during the year 1943, nearly twenty thousand people had contact with the offices of the Chicago Urban League. The organization was able to place about 50 percent of those people with gainful employment. Professor Green is the son of Little Rock Nine student Ernest Green and also the author of the 2007 book *Selling the Race: Culture, Community and Black Chicago, 1940-1955 (Historical Studies of Urban America)*.

"The Chicago Urban League met folks at train stations," said Andrea Zopp, the Urban League's CEO and President. Wilkerson writes that during meetings with newcomers, the urban leagues issued cards with warnings about not loafing, getting a job, not living in crowded rooms and not carrying on loud conversations in public places. Warnings also urged parents to keep their children in school and to not send for family members until employment was secured.

Green noted that during the years 1932 to 1960, 500,000 new blacks came to the city, including my parents. "There was a new African American coming to Chicago every forty-seven minutes [during those years]," Green said. He explained that Wilkerson's book is "epic" in its reach and sweeping narration of the Great Migration through the lives of three distinct families heading to Chicago, Los Angeles, and New York, respectively, because it told of a movement that "inspired actions and feelings of personal change."

When my parents left Mississippi and moved to Chicago around the spring of 1953, I am sure they didn't realize that they were a part of the Great Migration. However, history has shown that they were coming here for better opportunities. My father was in the U.S. Army, and we first stayed in what would then be referred to as a tenement near Forty-Eighth Street and Federal, situated near the city's Black Belt, which has been described as containing "the poorest neighborhoods of Chicago's South Side." Although my parents didn't settle in the Black Belt, any area in which my parents and others settled was among the poorest and most downtrodden neighborhoods. Substandard housing and poor infrastructure were the norm. It has been said that blacks who eventually ended up on the South Side were cut from a professional cloth and those who eventually settled on the West Side were working-class blacks. But my family's origins in Chicago were meager at best. My parents were not what you would have considered professional and certainly didn't belong to any black intelligentsia. It would be nice to spin yarns about my father hanging out with Richard Wright and others, but they were simply working-class folks.

My mother and father dressed to impress, circa 1953

Although many blacks who lived on the South Side during the early- to mid-1950s would align themselves with and be welcomed into the prestigious halls of the University of Chicago, research shows that many blacks who left their native homes and migrated to any of the Northern states were also better educated than most—and even better educated than the whites who arrived in these towns from other countries.

According to the Schomburg Center for Research in Black Culture, in some cities the black elite who were already settled sought to distance themselves from the newcomers, citing their lack of education and rural background. Black migrants responded to social isolation by forming communities that were comprised of people from the Southern areas they had left behind. In Northern cities, one could find blocks of people from the same general area of Georgia, Alabama, Mississippi, Louisiana, or the Carolinas. Throughout the urban North, the migration brought concentrations of African Americans, and the combinations of concentration and hope produced vibrant black communities. Unfortunately, due to many dynamics, these communities have been obliterated and/or are threatened today.

These things didn't play into my parents' decision to move to Chicago. Before they arrived here together, my father had followed his brothers up here, and he stayed a little while. My mother says that my uncle and his wife had property and they offered my parents a place to stay. Now, I don't know exactly if my uncle owned this property or was the manager for a white slumlord. But whatever his status, this put him a bit above the folks who were just renting. And albeit tenement-style living— where I am told that everyone living in the building, my relatives and my parents' newfound friends and their families, shared meals and babysitting duties, hand-me-down clothes, and other necessities—it was a wholesome, peaceful existence. This communal living had about four families living in large accommodations that were split to house more occupants than they should have.

My parents were in Chicago when my brother was born at Cook County Hospital. My father went on active duty in the military, and my brother and mother went back to Mississippi to stay with my father's family. After a year or so, my mother travelled with my father to California. He was re-activated, and my mother had my oldest sister, Audrey, at a military base farther North.

They settled back in Chicago after my father finished his enlistment— right back in the same apartment building on South Federal. Later, I was born at Cook County Hospital, where my mother said that the wards were segregated. My birth certificate says I was born in Ward Fifty-Four. It further records that my father's usual occupation was that of a factory laborer and my mother was a Negro. So I suppose it didn't matter what my mom did for a living, or it was assumed that she was a homemaker. A few years later, my sisters Phyllis and Olivia (Charise-Reese) were born.

Mom and family members, circa 1958

My father worked at Hygrade Meat Company, which was a good career at that time considering that Carl Sandburg once described Chicago as the "Hog Butcher for the World," with its stockyards and packinghouses, mostly located on the South Side. This proliferation of slaughterhouses was due to the mechanization of the processing of hogs before they were refrigerated by a technique refined by renowned Chicago industrialist Philip Armour. Salted meats, such as bacon and hams, were "packed" into barrels and routed to other nearby towns via trains, which were flourishing in Chicago.

Later, after exposure by novelist Upton Sinclair in his 1906 book *The Jungle*, which criticized the meatpacking industry, the nation would see its first pure food laws (FDA). Moreover, Chicago was near the center of most of the nation's meat production and near the center of its meat consumption; such a pretty spot in which to be situated. These jobs, and others in the railroad yards, steel mills, and other industries, paid wages far beyond what was available in the South.

Working in the slaughterhouse was described as dangerous, toxic, and brutal, but after awhile in 1959, my parents had saved up enough money to buy a single-family home in the Englewood community. It could be that my parents moved because of the construction of the new Dan Ryan Expressway, which prompted many blacks to relocate to different areas on the South Side. It's not that Englewood was an all-black community, as it appears to be now. Many whites still lived in the area, but most would be bitten by "white flight" during the next ten plus years, and they began to move to areas that were located even farther west. But blacks still weren't welcome in many locations on the South Side. Our house, which my father purchased for $13,000, was a three-bedroom "A-Frame" structure. It was my parents' first and only home, and I'm sure it was a great accomplishment for both of them. The house was right on the corner and had a gigantic "picture" or bay window, which proved the best spot to later watch the famous snowstorm of

1967, and a beautiful lawn surrounded by thick, lush hedges. It also had an enclosed back porch, pantry, living and dining rooms, as well as full kitchen, with a basement and attic, a black rotary dial phone, which stood on its own stand in the front of the living room. I call still recall one of our numbers GR6-4202 (the GR stood for Grovehill). There was only one bathroom for the entire brood. But the backyard was huge with an evergreen tree that is still thriving today, alongside the beautiful rose bushes that need little or no work to annually produce the prettiest roses ever!

In the 1950s and 1960s "concrete jungles" or high-rise buildings erected by the Chicago Housing Authority (CHA) provided public housing for thousands of black families on the South and West sides of the city. It is documented that there were already smaller public housing projects throughout parts of the city, but the U.S. Housing Act of 1949 released funding aimed at improving housing for those who were barely making ends meet. Some white aldermen didn't want the CHA to build public housing in their wards. Because of this, most of the buildings were concentrated on the South and West sides.

Why didn't we move into one of those buildings? The answer is simple. My father wanted a place for us where we could play outside in the backyard. He wanted to have his own property, where he knew his family would be safe and not have to live in yet another communal situation. Although the projects were nice and new and had flower gardens and community buildings, my father wanted something more substantial. So we got our backyard and our front porch. But he was dead set against us having any company or any business on the front steps. And that was the way it was, well into the 1970s. We rarely sat on the front steps to do anything. I believe he figured that it attracted too much unwanted attention. And even though there was a double swing set on the front porch, I only remember a couple of times sitting on that swing set. I do remember being "courted" by a young man when

I was a freshman in high school, and he and I may have sat out front a couple of times. But that was the culture of the day for working-class people and strong men like my father, who was working and raising his family. I am sure that the ban on hanging out on the front porch was for our protection, also. Can you imagine now going through Englewood streets, and other neighborhoods where there are backyards, and kids and families actually playing in them, as opposed to spilling all out on the front steps? Another factor in his buying a house was probably that my father's brothers and sisters were also buying homes and two-flats throughout the city.

One dismal reminder that a white family lived there before us was the brass knocker on the front door with the inscription "deliver all goods in rear." Now this could mean that the previous family felt that all service deliveries were better suited for the back door or it could have had racial undertones. Today, this reference to Negro deliverymen is totally ignored by the black family in the "white house," which is what others sometimes called our home. But my mother recently told me that a delivery guy knocked on the back door one day and, when asked why he didn't knock on the front door, he replied that he read the sign. I figured this delivery guy had to be young, to not realize that that sign was from another era.

Once you entered our home and went to the basement, you found a long, curving bar in the front room, and toward the middle was an old, big contraption, a Hercules brand furnace with a coal bin off to the side. For years, we enjoyed shoveling coal to dump in the furnace. We would get so dirty while playing in the coal bin after the coal was delivered by James Coal Company through the window. The window was situated right next to the coal bin and folded in so that the coal could be emptied into the basement. We would have fun going into the bin to shovel the coal closer to the front, because it had been dumped in one big pile. These deliveries were made regularly in the wintertime;

but if you didn't pay the bill, you didn't get any coal. "And if we didn't have enough money," my brother said, "We would have to shovel the coal from the sidewalk into the window, because the delivery guy would just dump it from the big truck and leave it there on the pavement."

We usually threw garbage in the furnace and even mice that we would kill after they occasionally scampered across the floors of our home. Once when we were teenagers, my brother was badly burned when he accidentally threw an empty paint can into the garbage can that held the clinkers or embers from the hopper of the furnace. It was a week night and my mother wasn't home. So it had to be a Wednesday—Bible study night—and my mother was at church. We heard a loud boom and the house shook a bit. We heard screams and my brother ran up the stairs, with the skin on his arm exposing the white meat, as the late comedian Bernie Mac would say. "I don't know what happened," Randy said, "I wasn't paying attention and had cleaned the hopper, because if you didn't clean it, the coal would back up into the hopper and cause a deadly exhaust. That was my job every night in the winter, but this time I got hurt."

My mother patched his arm up with salve and bandages, and I am sure cocoa butter, which was a main staple in our home during that time. I don't know whether we had health insurance or not, but my brother never went to the hospital. "I cleaned his arm and put ointment on it and then wrapped it up," my mother said. "No we didn't go to the hospital for treatment."

A central part of the beginning of Richard Wright's 1940 book *Native Son* revolves around the black character Bigger Thomas, a furnace, and a dead white girl. Years after this incident, when I read his book, which examined life on the South Side of Chicago, it quickly reminded me of our family's own furnace and coal bin. I guess for those living in apartment buildings, these things were irrelevant. But since we owned a home, we were used to all the elements that made it run more efficiently.

When we moved into our home my father was ambitious and enterprising, after having seen his brother manage his properties. My father decided to remove the old bar—which I'm sure had been host to many cocktail parties and many juicy conversations from the previous white owners—in order to construct living accommodations in the basement.

His eye was on the money because our home was only made for a single family, as opposed to many of the other dwellings on our block that were two- or three-flats. Two- or three-flat homeowners already had an instant revenue stream because they could accommodate rental families on one floor and live on the other. There was money to be made, as more family members arrived from the South who needed temporary lodging until they could get on their feet.

On the other side of the basement was the washing area, which also held the meat grinder that my father would use to grind meat and make sausages. We all knew how to work the washer once we became of age, but there was no dryer; we used clothes pins and clothes lines to hang and dry laundry. However, one time my mother had to play "she-ro" when my sister Phyllis was running clothes through the wringer and her hand became stuck. It took a very quick action of reversing that wringer and pulling my sister's hand out. I am sure our appliances were comparable to other families', but I do remember the day when we replaced the old gas stove and oven with a new gas stove that had a double oven, one on top and one on the bottom. We just moved the old can of used Crisco cooking shortening that was in the middle of the old stove and put it on the new stove. Crisco was another required staple, and once it was used for cooking and then melted, i.e., for frying chicken, it was poured back into the can for other culinary uses. Now my mother could have no excuse for not baking enough pies or cakes when the situation called for it. "Don't throw that grease away after frying bacon," my mother would say. "Just put the drippings in the Crisco can." It seems most stuff was fried back then. We rarely baked anything, not realizing the health benefits of baking and broiling. But somehow there weren't many chubby kids running around, and we got enough exercise by walking back and forth to school. We also had recess at school, which allowed us to release stress and also work off those pounds.

The block that we lived on at South Bishop Street was made up of many professions. There were teachers, policemen, bus drivers, and postal workers; all the good hearty professions of the 1960s and 1970s. There was even a family where the young lady taught ballet lessons in the basement. On the other block to our east lived a fireman and a distinguished physician. And down the block to the north lived the renowned jazz and modern dancer Darlene Blackburn, who formed a dance troupe that grew to achieve wide acclaim.

We attended public schools. However, not all the kids on the block did. There were some more fortunate—well with more disposable incomes—parents who sent their children to the Catholic school that wasn't far away, St. Raphael, which was located around Sixtieth Street and Laflin. Laflin is the street that is just to the west. It is also where the church is located close to everything—a church that has been there for more than ninety years. We had friends on Laflin, as a matter of fact, one of the families on Laflin had actually lived with us on Forty-Eighth Street and Federal. My father was known to everyone by his initials or some fashion of it—R.D. for Randolph but we secretly called him the "Warden" because he was stern, as fathers needed to be. By the 1980s, when my father worked with Latinos, they called him Art.

So what man with five children wouldn't have a car to go along with that nice, white house? And while my father had a few cars during our early years on South Bishop, one car sticks out with me more than others—that....

Three

1964 Red Buick

t's 1965, and it's time again for my father to purchase an almost new car. My father walks less than a mile from our home to Crown Buick Co. at Sixty-Third Street and Throop and buys a fire-engine red Buick Riviera. He had previously marveled at this beauty in the showroom. As he negotiates a price, my sister Audrey and I take advantage of a warm October day to walk to Coney Island at Sixty-Third Street and Ada, just west of Crown. Coney Island is the neighborhood fast food joint. (I guess it was named after the famous New York attraction). Well let me correct that: Coney Island is the place where the youngsters hang out. Nan's on Sixty-Third Street and Loomis, and later Red Apple on Sixty-Third Street and Ashland, which was owned by a former Sixteenth Ward Committeeman Jim "Bulljive" Taylor, and the Walgreens restaurant on the other corner catered to the mature crowd of this Englewood neighborhood. You see, during that time, as is now, the political machine in Chicago was in full throttle. Years earlier, Chicago was one of the first cities where blacks attained great political influence. Oscar DePriest became Chicago's first black councilman in 1915 and in 1928, he became the first black elected to the United States House of Representatives in the twentieth century.

As a matter of fact, blacks had won the official right to vote in 1965 with the Voting Rights Act, and local politicians and their cohorts were taking full advantage of this. It was common to have folks canvass in the community for whatever election was coming up, and my folks were active citizens in the process. It was a big thing to go up to the polling place with them, which was then located at the local elementary school. People would mill around, talking about one candidate or the other. So Taylor's restaurant was always crowded, with folks ordering fried chicken, chittlins, and whatever was the featured "bean" of the day, along with cornbread muffins, while discussing current political issues.

After the grown folks ate at the restaurant they could walk a couple of blocks and further enjoy themselves with liquor and other "packaged goods" from the Rothschild's, which was located on the southeast corner of Sixty-Third Street and Loomis. There was always some brutha in front of Rothschild's, who seemed to be drunker than the customers going in, who served as the doorman—in hopes of getting tips to buy more liquor. One such doorman was a man whose brother had recently been killed. When asked one day about his brother's murder, he shrugged his shoulders and said, "He's gone, but I'm still here."

My usual order at Coney Island is a burger and fries and, of course, a "suicide." A suicide is a soft drink made from a variety of the fountain flavors. My preference is more coke and orange flavors; something that I still order at the movie theaters even to this day.

"May I help you?" the clerk asked from behind the counter. "Give us two cheeseburgers, please," my sister and I both answered in unison. You see, we weren't twins, but we often behaved as such. The burgers came with fries at no extra charge. I mean most of the beef to feed the free world was being slaughtered right here in Chicago. So it was easy to come by.

As my father proudly deposits $400 on a nearly $3,163 debt—leaving him with a thirty-six-month, $77.60 note give or take—we reluctantly clunk down what seems to be a life savings of change for our food. As he drives past the Del Farm grocery store, also at Sixty-Third Street and

Loomis, reality hits him. He has to give my mother money for food. That's alright. We may have to eat beans and cornbread for a couple of days, but we are sure gonna look good in that red Riviera. That intersection is busy at this time of day. The rush hour buses running up and down the two streets take passengers either south on Loomis or west on Sixty-Third Street from the final stop on the "EL" line. Sixty-Third Street is the business district of this neighborhood. (Yes, this is the same Sixty-Third Street that the late Marvin Gaye sings about in *Hitchhike*).

Between Halsted to the east and Ashland to the west are a myriad of shops and restaurants that blacks are welcome to patronize. Throughout the years, Thompson's Barber Shop has also served as the local polling place at election time. A Mandl and Sons Cleaners advertises a "plant on premises." One of their specialties is blocking hats, and my father uses this service to clean his Dobbs hats that he most likely purchased at Howard Style Shops, down on Maxwell Street near Halsted—or what at that time was called Jew Town (to recognize the many shop owners who were Jewish). The shirts, suits, and dresses would always be so nicely cleaned and pressed. If you peered past the front counter, you could see the guy operating the pressing machine. This glimpse into the dry cleaning business would further manifest itself a few years later, as one of my father's brothers would open his own dry cleaning business over in the Gresham neighborhood. As teens we would hang out on a Saturday placing garments on hangers and pulling the plastic over each order to keep the clothes fresh and crisp. When you drive down Eighty-Seventh Street near Halsted you can still see the sign "Hegwood Cleaners" in the window.

Then there is Sarah's Beauty Salon, which is always filled with women vying to look beautiful, especially on the weekends. There are even two banks within this short area—Chicago City Bank and Trust Company and the Ashland and Sixty-Third State Bank, as well as a hospital named Englewood Hospital. The neighborhood to the west of Ashland is entirely white and even though our money is green, we are not welcome to shop there.

On our way back from Coney Island, with small, greasy brown paper bags and overfilled, brimming paper cups, we would spend the rest of our pennies on candy at Big Mama's grocery store. It takes us a while to arrive home, but it takes my father even longer. Although we live only moments from the car dealership, my father takes a leisurely drive home, beaming with pride every block of the way. This fond memory of the Englewood community will always remain in my heart, just as memories of my father and his new Buick always bring a smile to my face—a smile as wide as the grill on that bright, red Buick Riviera.

Englewood suicides.
Do or live.
Do or die.
Coca-Cola, 7Up and Sprite.
Carbon makes me feel alive, as my mother did with pops.
My mixtures are similar, riding the same streets.
As more thugs and more cops stop to patronize the pre-gentrified, and as the picture morphs.
And the rich get richer.
The poor get poorer.
And I am thankful to have lived up to, loved you, to have called you home.

-----Psalm One

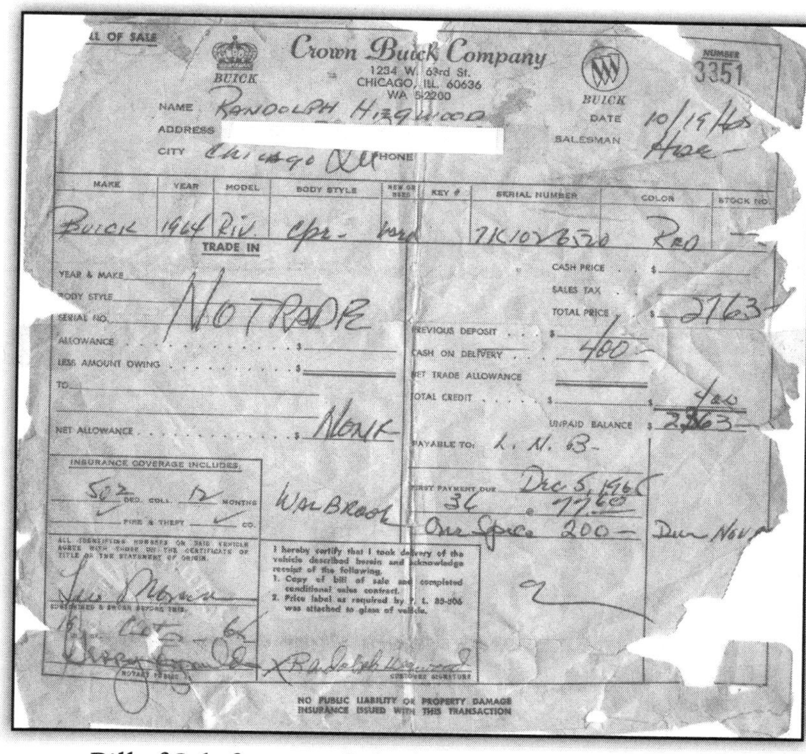

BILL OF SALE

Crown Buick Company
1234 W. 63rd St.
CHICAGO, ILL. 60636
WA 5-2200

BUICK

NUMBER 3351

NAME Randolph Higgwood
ADDRESS
CITY Chicago Ill PHONE

DATE 10/15/65
SALESMAN

MAKE	YEAR	MODEL	BODY STYLE	NEW OR USED	KEY #	SERIAL NUMBER	COLOR	STOCK NO.
Buick	1964	Riv	Cpe.	Used		7K1026520	Red	—

TRADE IN

YEAR & MAKE
BODY STYLE
SERIAL NO. NO TRADE
ALLOWANCE . . . . . $
LESS AMOUNT OWING . . . . . $
TO
NET ALLOWANCE . . . . . $ None

CASH PRICE $
SALES TAX
TOTAL PRICE $ 2763-
PREVIOUS DEPOSIT . . . $
CASH ON DELIVERY . . . 400-
NET TRADE ALLOWANCE
TOTAL CREDIT . . . $ 400
UNPAID BALANCE $ 2363-
PAYABLE TO: L. N. B.-
FIRST PAYMENT DUE Dec 5, 1965
36 @ 77.60

INSURANCE COVERAGE INCLUDES:
50 DED. COLL. 12 MONTHS
FIRE & THEFT CO.

ALL IDENTIFYING NUMBERS ON SAID VEHICLE AGREE WITH THOSE ON THE CERTIFICATE OF TITLE OR THE STATEMENT OF ORIGIN.

SUBSCRIBED & SWORN BEFORE THIS

NOTARY PUBLIC

I hereby certify that I took delivery of the vehicle described herein and acknowledge receipt of the following:
1. Copy of bill of sale and completed conditional sales contract.
2. Price label as required by P. L. 85-506 was attached to glass of vehicle.

CUSTOMER SIGNATURE

NO PUBLIC LIABILITY OR PROPERTY DAMAGE INSURANCE ISSUED WITH THIS TRANSACTION

Bill of Sale from my father's 1964 Red Buick Riviera

Four

My Red Car is Cooler Than Your Red Car – 1978 Red Pontiac

||||||||||||||||||||||||||||||||||||||||||||||||||||||||||||||||||||||||||||||||||||||||||||||||||||||||||||||||||||||||||

About twelve years after my father bought his red car, I bought a red car. But I needed my father's help—not with the financing—but his confirmation for me that this red car was well, in fact, a car. You see, my father worked at his regular job, but he was also a mechanic at heart. Often he would repair cars in the driveway and garage of our home. It was an old garage. The kind where you turned the lever and then used all your strength to push the door upwards. The garage held all types of tools that my father would regularly use to keep community members in their wheels.

When I decided to buy a car, it was kind of a tough job getting my father to take me car shopping. You see, he had one son and four daughters; so I guess the girls weren't supposed to drive—but eventually once we started working, all of my sisters purchased cars. My older sister, Audrey, darn near taught herself to drive, and when she was ready and had saved up enough money in 1975, she went to the local Ford dealership, which was located not too far from the house. She literally left the house, with Phyllis in tow, and they took the bus and came back with Phyllis driving the car that Audrey had just purchased. "I wanted to buy a car, but R.D. wouldn't teach me how to drive, so my cousin Henry took me out to practice and my younger sister drove it home for me," Audrey said. "At that time, Phyllis was the most skilled driver of all the girls." A week later Audrey received her driver's license, and she drove that white Granada with the red interior until the engine died in 1986. My younger sister, Olivia, purchased her first car—a bronze 1979 Pontiac Sunbird. She had taken a few driving lessons from Audrey and then rented cars to get extra practice. Eventually, she saved up enough money and bought her own car.

But I wasn't so lucky. I had gone to Jones and we didn't have driver's education. So when I finished high school in the early 1970s, I decided to take driving lessons from a professional driving school. Afterward, Henry's brother George took me to the DMV to get my license. But it would be years before I purchased an automobile.

After much prodding, my father did take me out car shopping. I had my eye on a Buick Apollo (I guess I figured if Buicks were good enough for him, then they had to be good enough for me). But that didn't pan out. I recall having left my job with the City of Chicago because of discrimination. Unfortunately I wasn't informed enough to sue them for such injustice. I had been passed up for yet another promotion within the Department of Water and Sewers. So one Friday in April 1977, when I found out that yet another secretary from the Bridgeport neighborhood had gotten the latest opening, I blew my top. For many years, the City of Chicago provided the students who were seniors from Jones with jobs to meet their course requirements and, after having worked there for a few years, I had been charged with training white girls who had come into the department.

At this point, I was really frustrated, and I went to my boss and told him that I had had it. I took off on that following Monday and went to Banner Employment Agency. I typed my butt off and took shorthand as fast as I could (all the good stuff I had learned in Ms. Henderson's class at Jones). I believe I was taking shorthand about one hundred and twenty words per minute for three to five minutes and typing well over one hundred words per minute for about the same length of time. Before

I could get home good, I received a call from Banner about an interview for the Roan & Grossman law firm, which was located downtown in the financial district. I accepted the position and now I was a legal secretary and making good money, but only one of two sistuhs there at the time. I first started off working in the real estate department and then I switched to domestic law. Since I thought I was important, I wanted to look important and decided it was time to get a car. Not that I would drive the car to work; it was crazy to tackle traffic and pay through the nose to park.

One day after work I took the bus to Rogers Pontiac in Bronzeville and salivated over a nice, shiny red 1978 Pontiac Firebird. My credit went through, as I had had smaller accounts at Lerner Clothing Stores and Carter's Jewelers on Madison and State. This is where I purchased my first real watch. I remember going into the jewelry store, which was very popular and situated on a busy downtown Chicago corner, picking out a watch, and being recognized as my father's daughter. "You are R.D.'s daughter, aren't you?" the clerk asked. I said yes, and she told me that she was related to one of my cousins. And she was—she wasn't just making small talk. She was the sister of my dear cousin Deloise, who at one time babysat us and taught us so many wonderful things.

But I couldn't buy a car that easily and I still had some reservations. I just wanted my father to look at the car for me—kick the tires, open the hood, anything. But he wasn't going for it and he kept ignoring my pleas. I felt defeated and just sat on the back steps crying one day and telling my mother that all I needed was for my father to check the car out. I didn't need money or anything. "Can't he come and just open the hood of the car and tell me it's an engine, let me know that it was a good purchase?" I asked my mother. So she intervened and told him that he had hurt my feelings by not going down to Rogers, which is still located at Twenty-Ninth Street and Michigan.

Let me interject here. My mother probably didn't say "hurt my feelings" because I can just hear you "old skool" folks exclaim, "What does she mean hurt her feelings? Your parents can't hurt your feelings. They can hurt *you* but *not* your feelings." Let me just say that she *suggested* to him that I was feeling really upset about this car situation. A few days later after I came home from work my father drove me down to the dealership, and shortly after that I was driving this sports car home, in my special "Driving Miss Daisy" style. The day I was due to pick up the car I took the bus down after work. After we completed the deal I needed to have them install the radio, and I was fine with waiting until the next day or so. But I was really stalling because it was nighttime and I didn't want to drive the car for the first time at night. The salesman insisted that I just take the car then and bring it back over the weekend. Well, I didn't know beans about the mechanics of a car, meaning that I had to figure out how to turn the lights on, etc., and figure out how to pump gas. I was a mess but I was triumphant and made it home in one piece. My father drove the car to work out in the south suburbs one day, and when he came home he said it was "too far down on the floor." Well, I'm thinking, "It's a sports car and not a Cadillac." I recall driving up the North Side on Lake Shore Drive or at many intersections and I would get looks from bruthas in their cars. They would all ask whether it was my boyfriend's car—not believing that I would own such a slick ride. No matter what I was thinking in my mind my car could still never have been as cool as my father's. "R.D. put his own record player in that Riviera," my brother would tell me years later. "He was a whiz with cars, and the record player was under the glove compartment and it played 45s."

My Firebird certainly didn't last as long as my father's cherry red Riviera. I moved away to Cincinnati and had to give the car back to GMAC (well actually, they had finally found out that I had stopped making payments, had left Chicago, and was working at Queen City Hospital).

"Hello, is that your red Firebird parked over there?" the security guard asked me one day as I was leaving work. I said, "Yes, it is." He proceeded to tell me that some guy in a truck had been checking it out. "Thank you, brutha," I said, extra grateful that he had clued me in. Shortly thereafter, I called the loan company and arranged to take the car to the nearest Pontiac dealership to turn it over. They were thisclose to repossessing it away from me. You may ask what was I doing in Cincinnati. During an episode called "life," I had been swept off my feet and headed there for what turned out to be a romantic adventure best discussed later.

Well, okay, since you and I have sort of become a bit closer during your time reading my essays, I will give you a little peek into this episode. The specimen was cool with this Ron O'Neal resemblance about him. He also lived on the South Side in Englewood, and he was cool enough to tell the strange guy who was seated at the table in the club that Friday night that he was my husband and that the "stranger" should find another table. "Not so fast, I was thinking." But it didn't bother me enough to ask him to leave, and the rest of the night at the Disco 10-8 on South Vincennes Avenue was quite nice.

We would later be married and ended up in Cincinnati for a while. Out of this union, we produced my lovely daughter, Cristalle Elaine Bowen, aka Psalm One. I was born prematurely, and I had to stay in the incubator for a while. As well, when my daughter came along in 1980, she was about five weeks early and weighed a mere four pounds, one-half ounce. She also had to stay in an incubator for a week before we could bring her home.

Cristalle's sudden birth sneaked up on me because I was going to a doctor's appointment and he immediately ordered me into the hospital. I was diagnosed with pre-eclampsia (a condition of hypertension) after a week or so of eating cold cuts and fast food because the cooking gas had been cut off in the far North Side building where my husband and I lived. I protested because there was a baby shower planned in my honor for the next day, but the doctor, John Strauss, M.D., wasn't hearing it. After a week of tests, an amniocentesis, and a crack at inducing labor, nothing yielded the desired results and a C-section was planned for the following week. And the rest—really this time—is history best explained some other time.

I just want something that reminds me of the hard work, the perseverance, the love.
It's something everyone wants, isn't it?
The ability to move about, to prove them wrong.
To drive down Lake Shore Drive with lookers-on.
I know you're trying to protect me, but sometimes all I feel is the rejecting that I'm older, and so are you, and we know it.
We're all materialistic.
We're all roped in saving pennies, dimes and dollars to taking my first car for a spin, holla!
My first was my aunt's last—an '87 Mustang.
It was mine.
It was fast.
So young and wide-eyed, surprised at life, why?
Now, finally, I feel I'm living it.
I'm in the driver's seat.
And all I need from you is this:
Tell me it's an engine.
Tell me it will get me to my destination in one piece.

-----*Psalm One*

Five

The Brougham (Bro-ham) Experience

||||||||||||||||||||||||||||||||||||||||||||||||||||||||||||||||||||||||||||||||||||||||||||||||||||||||||||||||||||||||||

During this time, my second to the youngest sister, Phyllis, was driving my father's Cadillac Brougham on a regular basis. I am not exactly sure what year it was, but the car did have a sunroof top—but no diamond in the back. Phyllis was also helpful with my father when repairs had to be made. He would call her to the driveway to operate the brakes or gas, as instructed, until a fix was found. You see, my father had to use the girls sometimes as he would have used a male child, since my brother was out numbered.

Phyllis was charged with driving that pimp car on Saturday mornings out to Blue Island to Gary Steel Supply Company, which was located nearly fourteen miles away, to where my father worked and where he and his co-workers shared a garden. Sometimes, she had to pick up the vegetables and bring them back to the house. She even drove herself to her Senior Prom, after her date had last-minute car trouble. Phyllis always said that this freedom in being able to drive and to drive such a bodacious car was a great treat for her. "I was tall for my age, and people automatically thought that I was older," she said. "I took pride in the fact that my father trusted me enough to drive the Brougham, and I boldly drove it to places other than that garden, whenever I had a chance." According to Phyllis, this responsibility also gave her a special connection to R.D., because she was the only child allowed to drive this car. She was so cool driving that car and she knew how to handle it, too. I'm sure you could catch her posing with a gangsta lean from time to time. It couldn't be helped driving such a massive beast! This experience helped Phyllis to become a great driver.

Around the time that we were in high school, my parents stopped renting out the downstairs apartment and moved down there themselves. Yes, we had the run of the upstairs, but that didn't mean much to four girls who would eventually start dating. We would have to get permission anyway to have any male friends over because we were respectable, church-going kids. I never crossed the line when it came to boys under the threat of, "If you get pregnant and have a baby we will put you out and you will have to rock it on the front porch." Now, is this the same porch that we could barely hang out on? How then was it that my father would force me to raise a baby out there? But it was enough of a threat to keep me chaste and clean and un-deflowered. And, besides, whenever we were seeing our company out, my parents could figure out just how long we lingered at the front door kissing or whatever.

Both parents would discipline us, with my father threatening to administer more whippings than he actually delivered. But the stern, ominous warnings, lectures or stares from him most times had more impact than the extension cord itself. Every black child knows that look—either coming from their father or their mother. And if they didn't, they would be better behaved kids if they did. Let me explain just as many black comedians have shared in their stand-up routines: If you did something wrong, your parents could just give you that menacing "I will knock your butt into next week" look, and whatever situation you were trying to bring would quickly be squashed. And, yes, we got the extension cord whippings! But we would prepare beforehand. If my father threatened to whip us after school we would pad ourselves with extra clothing—only to wait for nothing, a whipping that never came! No matter if we received our just punishment or not, we all lived to talk about it, and all five of us turned out to be pretty decent human beings.

Today my parents could probably get arrested for whipping us. But if the government had cause to intervene for what is considered corporal punishment or child abuse; conversely, the government should have given my parents a medal for raising four girls in the neighborhood without either of us becoming pregnant before we were married; and for raising a son who graduated high school and college and went on to make a good living for himself. Our parents used good old-fashioned work ethics and pooled their resources together for the good of their family. They both should also get credit for raising five children who have actively paid into the social security system and not lived off one government program after another. As a matter of fact, we all have college degrees and/or academic certifications that have contributed to our payments into this so-called "social security" system.

As I get older it irks me every time I see a "Prada-style" stroller on a CTA bus and see a young sistuh pushing that stroller with baby in tow, numerous shopping bags hanging off of the handles, weave laid just right, wearing every imaginable designer garment, with freshly manicured nails just glistening—often presumably supported by my tax dollars. And when the first of the month arrives and I am at the deli counter trying to buy just enough cold cuts to last while others are placing every type of ham in their already overstuffed shopping carts, I think, "Well, there is my social security. Hey, Mr. President, over here, what about me? I froze my fanny and fingers off, waiting hours in the cold for you to take the oath as the Forty-Fourth president. You promised hope and change." I guess that meant I better hope and pray—in case nothing changes—that there is something in the till for my social, physical, mental, and spiritual well-being when I retire!

Six

Early Education

||||||||||||||||||||||||||||||||||||||||||||||||||||||||||||||||||||||||||||||||||||||||||||||||||||||||||||||||||||||||||||||||||||

When we were in school, the schools were right in the neighborhoods. I can recall going to Copernicus, which was located around Sixtieth Street and Ada. I can remember sitting in the school yard at lunch time scraping the mayonnaise off the cheese sandwich that my mother had lovingly made. Many times we would have bolonie (bologna) that came encased in a red rind, which we would get from the neighborhood grocery store called Dosie's. Dosie's was located on the next block and my mother would send us there for bologna, cheese, bread, milk, Pepsi, and other items. We would sometimes run up a tab, if we were waiting for my father's payday on Friday. When my father got paid, we would take what we owed down to the store and pay the man. My mother loves Pepsi to this day. The bottles came eight to a cardboard carton, and we would take them back for the deposit. Funny, but I believed that the Pepsi would come back in the bottle, if you just let it sit there for a while. As well, I believed that there were actually little people in the radio who would talk to you—I couldn't imagine them being located in a studio somewhere. I mean, of course, the guys from WVON, which was known at that time as the Voice of the Negro, particularly Herb Kent talking about the "wahoo man" and the "gym shoe creeper," just had to be right smack dab in the middle of the radio. *Open Our Eyes* by The Gospel Cleffs is the song that Kent "The Cool Gent" would play to end his radio broadcasts at night.

Just as most urban cities had their own black, urban radio stations, WVON was and still is influential in the black community. Kent is a celebrated DJ who has been in the business more than sixty years and who knows his stuff. He still waxes nostalgic about years gone by and the celebrities he has met. While "jacking the dusties," he shares "infonuggets" that one would hope the young folks who might be listening will take in. Hopefully, they will come to realize and believe that their history is special—that they come from a proud people, whose ancestors would not be pleased with the state of affairs in black communities across Chicago and the country.

When George Gershwin Elementary School opened in the early- to mid-1960s, we all transferred to that school. There was a big procession for some of the students at Copernicus who were in the district for Gershwin, and we just marched right over to the new school, which was located at Sixty-Second Street and Racine. Years later, in a move to rename schools in black neighborhoods to promote black pride, Gershwin was renamed Granville T. Woods Math and Science Academy, after the man who sued to protect his invention of the telegraph.

During this time, the schools, as well as the city, were segregated and some black students attended classes in "Willis Wagons," so named after then-Chicago Superintendent of Schools' Benjamin Willis, who led the system from 1953 until 1966. According to the *Encyclopedia Chicago*, "Willis Wagons" was the pejorative term for portable school classrooms used by critics of Willis when they were protesting school overcrowding and segregation in black neighborhoods from 1962 to 1966. In December 1961, the Board of Education approved Willis' plan to buy 150 to 200 of the twenty- by thirty-six-foot aluminum mobile school units and install them at existing schools and on vacant lots. Besides installing the portable units, officials accommodated swelling ghetto pupil enrollments with double-shift schedules, rented commercial space, and much new school construction. Black parents, neighborhood organizations, and civil rights groups also urged authorities to permit black children to attend white schools with empty seats. Willis and the school board, however, resisted, preferring traditional neighborhood-based schools and refusing to reconfigure boundaries. Blacks countered with sit-ins, boycotts, and marches. The Woodlawn Organization claimed that it coined the "Willis Wagons" label in its one-day boycott of Carnegie School on May 18, 1962.

In August 1962, a *Chicago Crusader* editorial likened the education that white children were receiving in Chicago to that of a "plate brimming of molasses." But conversely, black children were merely handed a plate with a tad amount of molasses on it, with the plate tilted back and forth until the molasses covered the entire plate.

The injustices suffered within the Chicago school system were also heard across the nation. The *Saturday Evening Post* spoke out against them in July 1962 in an article titled "Block Buster," which reads in part, *"the Board of Education contributes to [block-busting] by writing off a school once it begins to change racially, consigning it to overcrowding, double shifts and supervision by the least experienced and lowest-paid teachers…if the dark American cries out to high heaven and marches to protest this cunning robbery before God and man, the protestation is branded as trespassing, he is arrested, handcuffed, jailed, indicted, while all the time taxpayers' money (and Negroes pay taxes) is being wasted on 'Willis Wagons' where education is spread thin."*

But the wagons were not to be stopped. In August 1963, the first Willis Wagons were erected near Seventy-Third Street and Lowe. It was not until March 1968, the *Chicago Crusader* reported, that black students were finally given the opportunity of equitable education, with the emergence of busing. "The white students tried to forget what they heard in their homes," the *Crusader* reported, "And the colored children remembered what they had been told by their parents—keep your head up high and pay them ignorant white folks no mind."

After graduating the sixth grade from Gershwin, I attended Beale Upper Grade Center for the seventh and eighth grades. Many friendships were made at this school, and I see people even today whom I remember as classmates, and we need only say "Englewood," and the connection or association is made.

Seven

Thanksgiving, Turkey, and Mogen David Wine

Holidays always meant a time for family. My mother had a brother named Eddie, who owned a grocery store and who lived on South Prairie Street. I thought he had a maid because his apartment had one of those old dumbwaiters, and there was always this lady there who served food during the holidays. I vividly remember having celery sticks stuffed with dressing, cream cheese, and crushed walnuts, and Mogen David wine, in the middle of a feast fit for a queen. Now just how our family ended up with a wine that has a Yiddish association is beyond me. As I researched the wine, I saw blogs and message boards where many people recalled it as being the "festive" wine served during their holidays, also. That lady whom I thought was a maid was really my uncle's wife named Fanny. My mother says Fanny was his common-law wife, but that distinction didn't matter to me. "Each year, Aunt Fanny's table would always be so formal," Audrey said. "I think that is why I have a formal table set up now, even when no one is coming over."

Of course, holidays were mostly always spent at home. If the entire family didn't visit relatives, we always dined at home. My mother would prepare everything, but we might help clean chittlins' or snap beans, clean greens, etc. After we all moved away, plans for a typical Thanksgiving dinner would start the week before. "Elaine, you're making the macaroni," one sister would telephone me. Sure, what else would I be expected to make? Years earlier, I had been crowned the "queen of macaroni and cheese." One sister would do the turkey, another the dressing, vegetables, and other dishes. While battling the crowds in the grocery store on Thanksgiving eve, I would vow each time not to wait so late the next year, simply so I could write a floating check prior to pay day. You see, back then, checks didn't clear as quickly as they do now. You could get paid on Friday but go into the store on the day before the holiday (Wednesday), write a check and not worry about it clearing before Friday morning. After everyone pitched in with cooking, on the blessed day, we would all gather, say grace, and take bets on whether my brother would show up on time.

My cool brother, Randy, circa 1975

But Thanksgiving 1988 goes down in history as the great revolt. Phyllis and I wondered, "Let's see how the British celebrate the holidays. We're going to London." We were met with opposition, however. "How could you not be here for the holidays?" we were constantly asked. Consequently, my pre-holiday week was spent ensuring passports were in order and trying to secure visas for a planned jaunt to Paris.

After what seemed like an eternity, even for a nonstop flight, we arrived at Heathrow airport in London. We were educated travelers, as we queued up to buy weekly passes for the Underground train system or what is locally referred to as the "Tube."

My sister seemed right at home. She worked for a British bank and had been to London before. She eats grilled salmon and at that time drank Stoli's; naturally she's cultured. We arrived at Victoria Station and walked over to the bed and breakfast. With little effort, I became acclimated to the reverse lane traffic. Hadn't I been to Nassau, Bahamas, a dozen times? But this was big time; I was in the home of Big Ben.

When we saw our accommodations—a cold room, with just barely enough space for two bunk beds and a water closet (toilet)—we shut the door and ran to the phone. We found another hotel not far away, and I insisted upon being shown the room before we booked. We stayed out as late as we could that first night and changed rooms the next morning after breakfast. Tuesday night after the customary tourist stuff, we had Johnny's Fish and Chips and wine for dinner at a private home. Wednesday night, I didn't find myself waiting in line to buy groceries but in the Windy City Bar and Grill eating ribs. For two sistuhs from Chicago, this was the next best thing to turkey.

Early Thursday, while my mother was probably having nightmares about macaroni and cheese, we arose and went sightseeing. After a couple of hours, I discovered that I had misplaced some money, and money and/or the lack of it can make you do crazy things. I was determined to cross this busy intersection with no clue as to how to maneuver around the traffic. After a while of jerking my head from left to right and a near collision with a double-decker bus, Phyllis decided to accompany me back to the hotel, where I retrieved my stash.

That year, I substituted a lovely homemade Thanksgiving dinner with all the trimmings for Harrods and shopping; Trafalgar Square and shopping; genuine "punks" and shopping; a session with Parliament and shopping; fish and chips and more shopping, and a gratis two-night stay at the luxurious Hyatt Hotel in Hyde Park and, of course, more shopping. Although I did miss the traditional Thanksgiving dinner, I would not easily trade the memories—only the excruciating flight back to the states.

But Thanksgiving, no matter where it is celebrated, has nothing on Christmas! During Christmas time, my father would go down to Fulton Market and buy fruits, nuts, candies, and other goodies for our home. Fulton Market was much like many markets in other big towns, where small stores would go to buy produce, fruit or fish. And the little guy trying to raise a brood of kids was also welcome to shop. During this season, the area would be filled with people from all over the city caught up in the holiday spirit—sort of like a scene from *A Christmas Carol* or from *If Scrooge Was A Brother* (a play performed by one of Chicago's black theater companies). But my father would also have enough to share with neighbors. Christmas circa 1966 also involved neighbors on our block going house to house and singing Christmas carols. The two evergreen or fir trees, one in the front yard and one in the back, would be decorated with festive lights that you could see from at least a block away. And the big snowman that lit up our entire front porch would be on display for all to see. Before we started using real Christmas trees, we would place the fake Christmas tree in the living room, decorate it and wait for the big, white Santa Claus (because this is all we knew) to come down the chimney.

We would leave milk and cookies out, and I guess my mother would come and take those away and place the presents under the tree. During these times, my siblings and I enjoyed games like Operation, Candyland, Twister, Etch a Sketch and Hands Down. These were all just simple things that kept our attention for hours, long before the electronics invasion.

One particularly nice gift was the big child-sized dolls that my older sister and I received, which even came with a hair dryer. We loved playing with the dolls. Although there was no selection of black dolls back then, it didn't matter. We just loved those dolls because we could play and pretend to have long, silky hair and nice lace dresses, just like them. Audrey still has her doll, even though there is an arm missing. My dear, late Aunt Olivia Shanks—my father's sister—and her husband, the Rev. Edward Shanks (whom we called Shanks), lived about three blocks from us. She made clothes for our dolls and chastised us when we didn't take care of them properly. She had an attic that she had converted into a tea room and set up with a few dolls sitting around as if they were drinking tea. My aunt also had a vast collection of Jet magazines in the back room, and as I recall we weren't allowed to handle them too much. We would have good times with my Aunt Olivia and Uncle Shanks. They would sometimes on Sunday take us down to Jew Town (Maxwell Street) to buy socks and other small items. I can remember going back to their house and eating smoked sausages. Our Uncle Shanks would spoil us more because my Aunt Olivia was real strict. Fondly, I do remember a Garfield Goose puppet that she bought me from the second-hand store named Value Village that was located near Sixty-Third Street and Ashland. She also bought me my first Girl Scout uniform, when I became a Brownie. "Make new friends, but keep the old, one is silver and the other is gold." I don't think I remember the Girl Scout pledge, but I do remember that song! Audrey also participated in the scouts for a short time, but she remembers that when it came to selling the cookies, my father wasn't too pleased with us peddling from door to door. "So, he bought all of our cookies," Audrey said. After she was grown, Audrey became a Girl Scout leader, and for many years helped other young girls grow into beautiful young women.

For them not to have any children, my Aunt Olivia and Uncle Shanks had the best toys, i.e., a vintage stereoscope viewer, where you would slide cards with pictures of different scenes on them in the front of the viewer and then look through the lenses to see what was basically a 3D effect. They also had a small cow box toy and when you turned it upside down, it would amplify the "moo" sound of a cow.

I suppose I should explain the term "Jew Town," lest I make enemies. The urban dictionary describes Jew Town as the Maxwell Street Market in Chicago, known thusly because of the predominance of Jewish business owners. It was an open air market; a precursor to Chicago's flea market. Anything that a person needed could be found on Maxwell Street (Halsted Street and Roosevelt Road). It is considered the birthplace of Chicago Blues and the "Maxwell Street Polish," and shopping there was quite popular.

My aunt is deceased now but I recently went over to my Aunt Lettie's home and on her living room table she, too, had Jet magazines strategically placed in a circular pattern, on display for all to see. Johnson Publishing Company, which was founded by John H. Johnson in Chicago in 1942, published Jet and Ebony magazines and they were a source of pride for blacks, as no other magazines covered and featured black culture as they did. People would scrape funds together to afford a subscription to this historical literature. This explains why the generation older than myself treasured these magazines and so proudly displayed them for all visitors to see.

As a matter of fact, Chicago was the launching ground for many businesses or services that were important to the black community, among them, the *American Negro Press*, which ran a black news wire service during the years 1920 to 1960, and Supreme Life Insurance Company, which was incorporated in 1919 by Frank L. Gillespie, an Arkansas native who built the company's headquarters in the Bronzeville neighborhood.

Eight

Blacks in White TV - Trying to Find a Little Color in a Black and White World

||||||||||||||||||||||||||||||||||||||||||||||||||||||||||||||||||||||||||||||||||||||||||||||||||||||||||||||||||||||||

While we enjoyed browsing the black-centered magazines while growing up, we didn't see many blacks on television. There were only a few syndicated shows that had black hosts or a majority black cast that weren't geared toward comedy or minstrelsy.

Of course, there was *Amos and Andy*, which ran on radio and television before my time. However, during the peak of racial turbulences in the late 1960s, some of which were brought on by the death of Dr. Martin Luther King Jr., television networks were eager to offer palatable programs featuring blacks that ran the spectrum of life from slum to suburb. And that's where *Julia*, with the elegant Diahann Carroll, came into play. This show aired from 1968 until 1971, with Carroll playing a beautiful young widow, employed as a nurse, living in an integrated apartment building with her young son. I loved this show and watching the young man Marc Copage who played her son, because he always seemed to call on or talk about his best friend and white buddy named Earl J. Waggedorn. Julia was a top-rated show when it first aired, even though it was politically critiqued. Some said that Julia's apartment, her occupation, and her life didn't depict what many Negroes were experiencing or living at the time. Whenever I see Carroll, I think back to my early teens and remember watching in awe, as she handled life and its unexpected crises on that groundbreaking television series.

Another favorite of mine was *Barefoot in the Park*, which starred Scoey Mitchell, who I thought was just so handsome, and Tracy Reed as a young, newlywed, black couple. It premiered in 1970 and Mitchell worked as an attorney. *Barefoot in the Park* was short-lived, but I always remember this show when I watch reruns of other shows like the *Dick Van Dyke Show* and see Mitchell in a role. I also remember watching *Get Christie Love* starring Teresa Graves as the first black woman to star in a network dramatic series—a distinction not met again until 2013, with Kerry Washington in *Scandal*.

Afternoons during our high school years were occupied with Barnabas Collins and Dark Shadows, which ran from 1966 until 1971, and the ubiquitous soap operas, including *One Life to Live*, *General Hospital* and *All My Children*. During this time, when it came to watching newscasts, there were not many black anchors. The few popular ones included Max Robinson and Carol Simpson. We were used to watching Fahey Flynn and Joel Daly for our local nightly newscasts, and they were charged with reporting the nightly news and especially that of Dr. King's death in April 1968.

A couple of years before his death, Dr. King made a grand attempt to integrate housing in Chicago. This move showcased Chicago for the racist town that it was—even more segregated according to Dr. King than he had seen in the South. The year was 1966, and with the large number of blacks who had and were still migrating to the city, equality was still an elusive ideal. History tells us that Dr. King moved to the West Side of Chicago, which was a mostly all-black area, but he organized a march for integrated housing on the South Side in the Marquette Park neighborhood. This is an area that wasn't far from where I first went to high school. This was a working-class neighborhood populated by immigrants from Poland, Germany, Italy, among other countries. The white protestors behaved like heathens, throwing rocks, blocking sidewalks, and rioting for hours, until police officers were able to disperse the crowds and lead Dr. King and his followers out of the area to safety.

"I do not imagine that the white and black race will ever live in any country upon any equal footing. But I believe the difficulty to be still greater in the United States than anywhere else."----- Alexis de Tocqueville.

Even with the above sentiment by the French historian who lived in the early- to mid-1800s, millions of immigrants still came to the United States, all presumably seeking better economic conditions, and many more seeking racial equality—an equality that was hard won and even today has escaped many because of their skin color. When Dr. King brought the Civil Rights Movement to Chicago, after all the marching and protesting in which he had participated in the Southern states, he was simply trying to right the wrongs of the Northern cities, just as he tried to right the wrongs down South.

Riots were not uncommon, but at one point the riots took on a different composition and blacks began rioting for better conditions within their own neighborhoods. They destroyed white-owned businesses and their own enclaves in the process. In many cases, it took decades for some neighborhoods to be restored—if at all. After significant riots in cities beginning in 1965 in the Watts area of Los Angeles, Chicago, Newark, and another particularly devastating riot that occurred on July 23, 1967, in Detroit, the Kerner Report, named after then-Illinois Governor Otto Kerner, investigated the reasons behind these civil disturbances. The report—conducted also with help from Mayor John V. Lindsay of New York City—came out shortly after Dr. King's death in 1968 and charged, among other things, that local news segments were distorting the news in urban black communities. The protests against segregation and discrimination, previously limited to radio broadcasts, were now more impressively shown in the form of televised accounts. William Small, in his 1970 book *To Kill A Messenger: Television News and the Real World*, describes scenes of young Negroes dragged out of buildings, grim-jawed, sit-ins surrounded by angry whites, and police moving in with brutal swiftness. Under the auspices of Pres. Lyndon B. Johnson's

National Advisory Commission on Civil Disorders, the report revealed the following regarding disturbances the year before Dr. King's death.

"We have found a significant imbalance between what actually happened in our cities and what the newspaper, radio and television coverage of the riots told us happened. The Commission, in studying last summer's disturbances, visited many of the cities and interviewed participants and observers. We found that the disorders, as serious as they were, were less destructive, less widespread, and less a black-white confrontation than most people believed."

The report went on to cite among the reasons for the violence: *"The most fundamental is the racial attitude and behavior of white Americans toward black Americans. White racism is essentially responsible for the explosive mixture, which has been accumulating in our cities since the end of World War II."* The report's most profound passage was: *"Our nation is moving toward two societies, one black, one white—separate and unequal."*

After these revelations, recommendations were made to improve living conditions in the so-called ghettoes and to offer more employment opportunities. But even after Dr. King's death, more rioting broke out in cities, especially Chicago. However, one good outcome of the Kerner Report was that more blacks, among them local Chicago journalists Bob Petty, Merri Dee, and Warner Saunders, were hired in newsrooms around the country. Now, blacks could see more of those who looked like them reporting the news, and not just on the television sit-coms. Sadly, however, decades later the news reports, whether delivered by black or white anchors, is disheartening and full of daily shootings and criminal acts. "Men are made to live together as brothers," is a quote attributed to Dr. King shortly before the March on Washington in 1963. After so much "black-on-black" crime, this could sadly apply solely to black bruthas and sistuhs and not to whites and blacks, as Dr. King meant at the time.

Nine

Food and Rations

M y father and his brothers made frequent trips back down to Mississippi. When they would come home, they always returned with watermelon, greens, pecans, fruit, and hogs from the family farm. Sometimes, Phyllis, my mother, and Olivia would accompany my father. The three would get lunch boxes or shoe boxes packed with enough food to last until my father could stop for gas. As long as my father had his coffee and his cigarettes, he was fine. But I am sure there was enough chicken for everybody. Phyllis recalls how the driving was a pain, but they had so much fun. And once they arrived in Shaw, Mississippi, the trips were well worth it, especially when they returned home with the spoils from the excursion.

When it was time to turn the peaches or pears into preserves, my sisters would assist my mother with the long process. After peeling the fruit, my mother would put it in a huge pot, adding sugar and cloves, allowing the fruit to sit for at least two nights. Afterward, a little bit of water would be added, and then the pears would be cooked slowly for about ninety minutes until they reached the consistency for preserves. With the Mason jars at the ready, after they had been sterilized with hot water, the fruit would be transferred to the jars. With juices running down the sides, the orange-colored bands would be clamped around the jars before the tops were put in place. After the jars cooled down, the tops would be tightened and the jars would be labeled and stored in the pantry. If you didn't have the bands or the jars were stored without the tops being fully tightened, the fruit would spoil.

The smells from the cloves and the fruit are something that I can recall as I am writing this. They permeated the house. And no matter in which direction you turned the jar, you could still see the black cloves. The fruit was used for just good eating or, in the case of the peaches, for peach cobblers in months to come. My mother would portion out the flour, sift it onto the counter, and afterward begin to use the big, heavy wooden rolling pin to roll out the dough. She would then prepare the baking dish, fill it with the homemade pie mixture, trim the dough that hung over the edges, and use her thumb to crimp the dough to seal it to the baking dish—while not forgetting to poke tiny holes into the top of the dough. Those peach cobblers would be so flaky, sweet, and delicious.

We are now all set for dessert, and on the protein side my father would take that nasty looking hog and section it out. But one day the hog came to life!

Hey, you, cutie, yeah, you with the short plait that looks like my tail, can you help me out? the hog asked, while spread all out on the board. Since Chicago is the 'hog butcher' of the world, why couldn't your crazy uncles find any pigs right down the street? This hog wouldn't dare insult your father in his own home! You live on the South Side, and I am sure there are plenty of hogs around down at the Stockyards. Why did they have to cash their checks, load up the Cadillac, and put on their best 'union' clothes and come down South to upset my happy home?

Well, I was flabbergasted and about to high-tail it out of the kitchen. But this brutha's story was interesting and I needed to hear more.

Get me out of here, please. Give me mouth-to-mouth, he said while winking. Breathe some life into me, so I can just pack my bags and get the train home.

I have family at home, just like you guys. Let me introduce myself, as he pulled out family photos. My name is Porky, and my old sow's name is Bess. And I have little piglets at home, too. One of them, named Sissy, is sassy but very talented. She sings and dances and hangs out with stuffed animals. I know she will make it big one day. And I have a son who sits and watches cartoons all day. He doesn't go to school but dreams of being on the big screen himself. My ol' lady is probably looking for me about now. I left Jody the pig with her, since he's younger, but I don't think I can trust that swine. He has a reputation. Maybe we can make a trade for some nice, plump chickens or a nice, thick side of beef. Please, let me outta here!

But no, I wasn't hearing anything that nasty hog had to say. We had to eat, and I knew the swine would eventually be processed and cooked, providing many meals and treats for my family. It was time for him to be sectioned off in the name of—well just in the name of my family— and take his rightful place in our deep freezer. So try as he might, the hog couldn't escape his fate, and afterward my father would grind some of the meat in the meat grinder that was in the basement. And we kids anxiously awaited the best part—the pork rinds.

My father was a cook in the U.S. Armed Forces, and The Quartermaster Corps proudly issued Private Randolph Hegwood an official commendation on June 11, 1954, that certified that he had satisfactorily completed the "Course of Instruction in Cooking Course 10-E-18 MOS (1824)" in Fort Leonard Wood, Missouri. At home, he would make the best homemade donuts—especially glazed. These donuts would go well with the Maxwell House coffee that we ALL had to learn how to make. You would put the coffee grinds in the top of the aluminum coffee pot, and you would run water through it and percolate it on the stove. And if you got it wrong, well, "You go to school everyday, and you don't know anything," is what you would hear my father say. At a young age, Audrey was so fascinated with the porcelain coffee cup that she attempted to pull one off the table one day. She was scalded with the coffee and the scar is visible to this day. Again, I don't think she went to the doctor.

I am sure my father probably blamed this accident on my mother. You know, as families worked the best, the father had the financial responsibilities, and the mother took care of mostly everything else. So I can hear my father say, "Pinkie (but the "i" would be pronounced like a long "a"--Pankie), you done messed around and let that girl burn herself, or you done messed around and let that girl get hit by a car, or you done messed around and let that girl fall off the porch, or you done messed around and let that boy burn his arm off." By the time the television series *That Girl* premiered in 1966, we girls thought that they had named a show after us. Then R.D. probably would have said, "Pankie, you done messed around and let them name a show after my girls, good job!"

Even though my father could chastise you with a razor sharp tongue, if you woke up early in the morning to go to the bathroom that seven—count them seven—people shared, you would lovingly see him, with his slight frame, sitting at the window, maybe in his boxers, smoking a cigarette with the other hand to his head, as if he were thinking out the day, and other times with a cigarette and coffee steaming from his white porcelain, coffee-stained cup.

However, any chastisement he may have dished out was long forgotten when you dived into a dish of his famous homemade vanilla ice cream during the summer cookouts. It started out with some rock salt, ice and cream, all cranked by hand in the rusty, mint green contraption that we knew as the ice cream maker. After he cranked a bit, everyone would get a chance at cranking—sort of like equal opportunity ice cream making—until the ice cream was firm enough to eat, right there on the spot! The Good Humor man had nothing on my father when it came to his nice, creamy summer treat.

This would keep everybody busy, until the ribs and the hot dogs and hamburgers were ready on the grill. My father would always get the meat just a bit crispy. You know how some upscale bar-be-que restaurants now advertise "burnt ends?" Well, we had burnt ends back in the day whenever my father cooked, and they were just as good as any made now on a Weber grill.

Farm hands, something I wish for
In a world of chemical food dependencies, we have the tendencies
to eat what isn't keeping us healthy.
As Whole Foods prepares to invade, I reminisce with mom about past days,
where trips to the South meant more than hand to mouth.
Times of my grandfather, preparing meats, treats and feats, largely unknown
on these current Englewood streets.
Just a budding leaf, a sprig of life, a rose from concrete, a tale of two
Englewoods, of two lives, of wishes on the corner of our home.
If we are to call my granddaddy R.D., the Mayor, then Pinkie is First Lady.
Taking lessons from the 50s, 60s and my introduction, the 80s.

-----Psalm One

Ten

Buttermilk and Cornbread – A Working Man's Crème Brûlée

One of my father's favorite treats was buttermilk and cornbread. I have never tasted it and while I do enjoy cornbread, I never acquired an affinity for buttermilk, so I haven't a clue as to why he liked it so much. But there he would go. After my mother would make a cast iron skillet full of cornbread, my father would sniff out some leftovers to make what I called "ghetto crème brûlée." Since I don't know, and I didn't put much research into it, I presume that this is a Mississippi thing. I am almost certain that my father didn't first eat this….er… delicacy on Forty-Seventh Street at Geri's Palm Tavern or at one of the other happening clubs on the South Side.

First, he would crumble a large portion of cornbread in a bowl and then he would pour buttermilk over it, until it covered the cornbread. For good measure, he would top it off with a bit more buttermilk and sometimes sugar. Now, when I asked family members about this "next big thing in desserts," I did learn a few things. Namely, Phyllis would also eat this wonderful dish with my father, while they both watched *Gunsmoke*, which originally began as a radio program. Now, even for a young girl, not yet smitten by boys, I thought that Marshal Matt Dillon, played by James Arness, was a nice looking guy. And there was always an occasion for him to shoot somebody in front of the OK corral, while his sidekick Festus, played by Ken Tucker, tried to figure it all out. And I just knew that Matt Dillon and Miss Kitty, the sassy, mole-wearing saloon owner played by Amanda Blake, had more of a thing going on than what we saw on television.

For Phyllis, watching Matt Dillon made the cornbread and buttermilk even easier to swallow. "Well R.D., although a great defender of the fold, wasn't a warm and cuddly type; so if eating cornbread and buttermilk made me a favorite child from time to time, then so be it," Phyllis said. "The cornbread was pretty tasty and easy to swallow, but the challenge as a young girl was gulping down that sour tasting buttermilk that made me gag."

Phyllis said there would be many times when she and my father would watch television and eat their "ghetto crème brûlée." But her favorite *Gunsmoke* snack was the freshly popped popcorn that he would pop with cooking grease and salt. It was nice and hot, and each kernel was perfectly popped and poured into a big bowl. Yum yum!

My father with his crème brûlée

Eleven

Gym Shoes, Blue Jeans and Gear

||||||||||||||||||||||||||||||||||||||||||||||||||||||||||||||||||||||||||||||||||||||||||||||||||||||||||||||||||||||||||||||||||||||||||||||||||

While growing up, going to school meant you had maybe three pairs of shoes—a pair of gym shoes, a pair of school shoes, and one pair of dress shoes that you mostly just wore to church. If there was a special event at school, the girls would put on a freshly starched dress and either anklets or bobby sox with our dress shoes. The school shoes might invariably be Buster Browns or Saddle Oxfords. We didn't have Nikes or Air Jordans. There were really only a couple of brands of shoes that were popular with teenaged boys, and those were Chukka boots (which we also called desert boots) and a nice little gym shoe called Converse. Converse shoes were not priced so insanely high that one kid would beat up another kid or shoot another kid to take them. We would shop for most of our gym shoes and blue jeans at Bill's, which was located—again—right around the corner on Sixty-Third Street and Laflin. When we got fancy shoes my mother would take us to Wieboldt's or Sears, and we would actually get our feet measured for the right size. We didn't have money to waste so there was no buying a pair of shoes and NOT wearing them because they were ill fitted.

When my younger sisters were going into high school, I was working, and I recalled playing big sister and taking them on the bus to the River Oaks Shopping Center, in the south suburb of Calumet City. This was considered a special treat for them: No. 1, because we were all going out of the neighborhood to shop; No. 2, we were taking the bus; and No. 3, their big sister was going to buy them clothes. The River Oaks Shopping

Center is a huge shopping mall, located about eighteen miles from where we lived. It took us four buses to get there, but it was worth the trip. It was sort of like the credit card commercial that lists certain items and the last is "priceless." Well, that explains the smiles and gratitude that Phyllis and Olivia had once we were finished shopping. It was nice to be able to treat them and for them to start high school wearing the latest fashions. The ultimate joy of this experience was being able to help my parents out by footing the bill.

Twelve

Have You Got Good Religion? Certainly Lord!

||||||||||||||||||||||||||||||||||||||||||||||||||||||||||||||||||||||||||||||||||||||||||||||||||||||||||||||||||||||||||||

Y ou knew I couldn't write a book of essays on black life in the 1960s and 1970s without a chapter on religion and churches. Churches have traditionally been the foundation of the black community, and Chicago has held prominence as having churches that played a great part in history—not just in the city, but on national and international landscapes. In the 1930s, Thomas A. Dorsey the "Father of Gospel Music" created the sound that became known as Gospel from inside the famous Pilgrim Baptist Church. Albertina Walker, Mahalia Jackson, Aretha Franklin, Sallie Martin, James Cleveland, The Staple Singers, and The Edwin Hawkins Singers are among those who have performed at the church. Pilgrim, which was nearly destroyed in a 2007 fire and is being reconstructed, also hosted the funeral of boxer Jack Johnson in 1946. Dr. King also delivered sermons at the church during the height of the Civil Rights Movement.

The first church that I remember going to as a kid was the Old Ship of Zion Missionary Baptist Church, which was located around Forty-Seventh Street and Wabash. It was close to where my family first lived; and even after we moved to Bishop Street, we continued to attend services there. On Sundays, when my father didn't take us, my mother would dress us up, walk down to Sixty-Third Street to catch the bus going eastbound. I am sure we resembled a mother and her ducklings walking down the street, and I am sure there were many other families

58

doing the same thing on Sunday mornings. When we reached State Street, we would switch to another "big green" CTA bus and head north, until we reached Forty-Seventh Street. We would then walk over a block to sit in church and hear what the esteemed "mand" of God, the Rev. Bruce Clady, had to say in his sermon. In the summers, we would often have picnics in the church parking lot after services. Whenever I hear Wynton Marsalis' *In This House, On This Morning*, I think of those days in the parking lot with the picnics and kids just playing, without a care in the world. Marsalis' entire two-CD set is playing out a church service—from devotional to pot-blessed dinner. Although we lived within walking distance of a church, Trinity Missionary Baptist Church, we still attended services at this one a few miles away. Eventually, however, our family became members at Trinity. Now there were other churches in other neighborhoods. But our "Trinity" wasn't Trinity Missionary Baptist Church No. 1 or the Original Trinity Missionary Baptist Church or the New and Improved Trinity Missionary Baptist Church; it was just plain old Trinity Missionary Baptist Church. And for those of you who are wondering, our "Trinity" was not the church that Pres. Obama once attended. By choosing Trinity we had no excuses. Then, we "ducklings" could fall out the back door of our home and fall into the back door of the church, which was led by the Rev. Albert Wilson.

We had such fun at Trinity and we learned and were nourished in the community not only by our parents and other church members but at that time by each and every parent in the neighborhood. "Aunt Bessie," who wasn't really our aunt, lived around the corner from us with her sister's family, and she could see everything. Even with no cell phones or email if we did something on Laflin Street that didn't sit right with her, then my parents would find out in due time. And their punishment would sometimes come after Aunt Bessie was through with us. We couldn't complain, and my parents probably wouldn't have heard it anyway. Back then, it took a village and the little villagers (hard-headed, nappy-headed, big-headed Negro children) just went with the flow.

The first lady of the church, Mrs. Mayola Wilson, was a preacher's wife in the old-fashioned vein. She taught arts and crafts, sewing, etc., to the young kids in church. In the rec center, which was located next door, there was a pool table, sports equipment, etc., for not only the church members but also neighborhood kids who would come in to while away the time. We weren't out shooting each other or doing drugs. And this was a time rich in the Motown Sound, so it was customary to watch the younger kids play games and the older teens listening to Smokey, Stevie (do these guys need last names?), the Temptations, the Supremes and Marvin Gaye, among others. Not that all kids in Englewood were angels, because certainly there were gangs at that time, but the rec center served as a refuge.

The prevalent gangs in the neighborhood during that time were the Satan Lovers and the Disciples. But try as they may to recruit my brother, my father stood firm against any gang recruitment involving my brother. And if there was a fatality, as when a young man named Chuckie was found dead in the back alley a few doors down from our home in the early 1970s, it was all kinds of news—not just another shooting as we see today. During the church's annual "Heaven and Hell" party, church and community members would, of course, attend, but word would travel throughout the community, and the doors on that particular Friday night would also welcome gangbangers from both affiliations. There were never any disturbances that I can recall. It was a kick seeing how many people would choose to eat from the "Heaven" side, which had white cake, punch and probably sandwiches. If you ate from the "hell" side, you received devil's food cake, chili and still probably punch. Most of the thug types in the neighborhood would go for the "hell" side, and, of course, the girls who liked the "rough necks" would also meander over to that side. These parties were held in the church basement. I recall having church dinners down in the basement, too, with the industrial-sized stove, whose pilot light had to be lit by a grown up. Whichever auxiliary was in charge that Sunday morning would cook the customary fried chicken, macaroni and cheese, potato salad, accompanied by greens or green beans. Of course, there were desserts like German Chocolate Cake or pound cake that members would bake at home and bring in. The congregation would be served, and afterward the kitchen and basement would be cleaned up as shiny as a whistle.

We were all baptized in the church, in the baptismal pool that was located near the front. Everyone would get dressed in all white and the girls would wear a swim cap, lest their freshly pressed hair would get wet. Before gently pulling you down into the water, as you held your nose for safety reasons, the Rev. Wilson would say, "Obedient to the Great Head of the Church, and upon the profession of my faith in Him, my (brother/sister), I indeed baptize you in the name of the Father, and of the Son, and the Holy Ghost." And down you would go, emerging as white as snow, or so we believed. During the entire ritual, the choir would sing, "Take me to the water, take me to the water, take me to the water, to be baptized. None but the righteous...none but the righteous..." Most times, all the mothers of the pre-teens or teens being baptized would "catch" the Holy Ghost afterward, with much jumping and praising God for what they believed was cleansing the new saint's soul and delivering to them a supposedly obedient child. I didn't mind this ritual, even if at the time I might not have fully understood it.

Afterward we would get dressed again, either putting on our white socks or carefully placing our white stockings on our legs—after applying enough lotion or Vaseline to make us shiny again—and splashing on a bit of Chantilly perfume that we had bought by the big bottle for $5 at the local Walgreens. And when pantyhose became fashionable, we learned to place those over our freshly shellacked legs, also. We even learned to buy shades other than white or coffee. But for a long while, it was either white or coffee stockings, paired with that troublesome garter belt.

As well, I didn't mind being at church all day; and as teens we often got on the church bus in the evening to visit other churches, notably, Mt. Pisgah and the historic Fellowship Missionary Baptist Church. Back then when the preachers took up collections, they would almost literally go into someone's wallet and get the cash that was needed to make the official offering. "Come on Brutha Larry, I know I can count on you for $20," the preacher would say, while dipping his hand into Brutha Larry's wallet.

At Trinity there was the Mother's Board, the Usher Board, Vacation Bible School, Baptist Training Union, the Youth for Christ group, the senior choir, the children's choir, and the youth choir. The celebrated choir director at one time was Reuben Lightfoot, and he had the Victory Choir rocking at the morning service, which required two "passings of the plates," and the evening service. All of my sisters were in the choir at one time or another. The choir members would come down the middle aisle of the mid-sized church in white, flowing gowns, swaying and marching to whatever Gospel song was most popular at the time. I couldn't sing a note, so I stayed away from the choir.

My youngest sister loved the spiritual nourishment that she received at church so much that today she is founding pastor of her own church, Chicago-based Generational Blessings Family Worship Center. My mother encouraged her to nurture this gift when she was a teenager. She is the epitome of a pastor who often cares more about her congregation than she does for herself. "Going to church was my favorite pastime as a child," Olivia said. "I looked forward to the many programs offered at Trinity for children. As a teen, I looked forward to the Bible teaching and fellowship that followed each service." Olivia added that even back then she had the desire to go to church every day and did as often as my father would let her. "Sometimes, after being denied his permission, my mother would entreat him on my behalf, and I would ultimately be allowed to go to 'revival'," Olivia said. "I would hasten to make that phone call, arranging a ride and waiting at the picture window for the church van. Revival was supplemental to Sunday service. Back in the day, revival was conducted for a 'week's length' at a time, Monday through Friday, and was designed to spiritually refresh, renew and inspire those who attended."

Olivia attended revival almost every day of the week during her latter teen years, all the way into adulthood. "It prepared me for my pastoral ministry, which focuses on accepting Christ and re-establishing and restoring the family unit as God ordained with the husband leading his home spiritually and providing for his family naturally," she said. "Though family life on Bishop Street was not nearly perfect, it was solid. My father taught me a tremendous work ethic; he was a hard worker and great provider. My mother taught me to love Jesus and His people with all of my heart and that serving people is serving God."

Along with leading Generational Blessings, Olivia has partnered with and serves on many organizations, including the Chicago Bar Association's Interfaith Committee. She has played a significant role in creating a restorative justice program that is taught in elementary schools, teaching fifth- through eighth-grade students how to resolve conflicts peacefully. Olivia also teaches much needed etiquette classes in local schools. These are things that we were taught but that are missing in schools today.

My mother has been at the same church for more than fifty years and she still sings in the choir. She has that same spirit and devotion as always, but many women at church don't rock the hats as they once did. Back then, she and the other women would wear such fabulous hats. My mother would buy her hats from Ms. Lillian, who came door to door to sell her fine pieces. My mother said that Ms. Lillian bought her materials from Fox Millinery, which was located downtown at State and Lake Streets. Ms. Lillian was a sharp dresser who came to the house every Saturday morning with a large bag, which seemed larger than her because she was small in stature. "She would be sharply dressed, wearing a hat of her own design, jewelry and rings on her fingers, makeup on her face, looking good so early in the morning," my mother said. "Ms. Lillian made fabulous hats, and whatever you envisioned, she could design it for you at reasonable prices."

Her peak seasons were around Easter and Mother's Day and she even accepted layaway. Ms. Lillian would come with hat boxes and my mother would "oooooh" and "aaaaaah" over them, trying to figure out just how much money she would need to put one in lay-a-way when she didn't have the money to just buy one right on the spot. After a couple of weeks, my mother would be able to wear the hat to church on communion Sunday, which is the first Sunday of the month. A nice white hat, with a lacey veil hanging off the brim would go nicely with the nice white suit and white shoes that my mom would wear to church. White represents the color of purity and back then, you wouldn't dare wear any color other than that on the first Sunday. "When I would proudly wear one of her hats to church, I knew that no other woman would have on a hat nearly as fine as mine," my mother said.

During this time from the early 1960s to the mid-1970s, even though the merchants didn't have brick and mortar stores, these door-to-door sales were a way of keeping the economy pumping and of keeping the money made by blacks in the black community. This was not a practice of discrimination, as some may think, but of supporting businesses and not having to buy from white merchants, who would just as soon not have us patronize their stores anyway.

Later on Saturday night, all the kids would take their baths, because there would be no possible way to accommodate all of us on Sunday morning. But before we took our baths, we would all crowd around the television to watch Saturday night religious programming, which consisted of watching Isabel Joseph Johnson on the *Rock of Ages* hour, with regular commercials from the A.R. Leak Funeral Home. This funeral home was "founded by God" in 1933 and was the subject of a *Crain's Chicago Business* video series in August 2013 that detailed the firm's long-term commitment to serving the community with dignity. The story also outlined the fact that the A.R. Leak Funeral Home (now called Leak & Sons Funeral Homes) handled the arrangements for one-fifth of the more than 500 homicide deaths in 2012. Many of these funerals were for victims of the escalating black-on-black crime that has swept through the city, including women and children. During these *Rock of Ages* broadcasts, Joseph Johnson could wear some hats, which I gather she probably bought from Ms. Lillian, also! Other Saturday night treats would be to play the "hi-fi" and listen to Gospel music and sermons like *Dry Bones in the Valley* and music from James Cleveland.

The Father, Son and Holy Spirit.
So close to God, so far and so near Him.
My Englewood was a Mennonite church.
My Trinity was an awesome Trinity.
Fellowship, learning…and…music.
I'll be honest with you…
If it weren't for the wonderful messages given to us through Gospel music, I wouldn't have wanted to go.
There isn't any genre of music more beautiful.
And my love of the Most High is analogous to my love of music.
It's why I have a biblical rap name.
My fellowship has been playing drums for the choir, for singing his praises.
For cultivating the gifts He has given me.

We are a blessed people!
From Englewood, from Trinity, from Strongtower.
Thank you every day.
Thank you for every Sunday.
Thank you for a praying grandmother and earnest aunts.
Thank You.

-----Psalm One

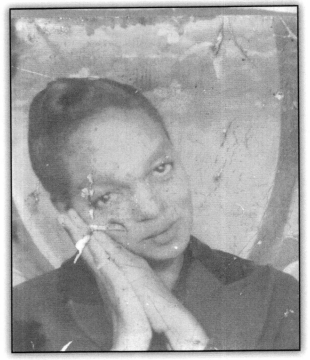

My mother strikes an angelic pose, circa 1951

Thirteen

Block Clubs, Block Parties, and James Brown

|||||||||||||||||||||||||||||||||||||||||||||||||||||||||||||||||||||||||||||||||||||||||||||||||||||||||||||||||||||||||||||||

Into the mid-1960s to the mid-1980s the families on our block were part of an active neighborhood Block Club, and with this came many parties where the street would be cordoned off and little babies and young teens could play in the street without threat of getting run over by a car. There would be games for kids, ball playing, food, and music from James Brown, Stevie, and Aretha blasting to the high Heavens. There would be the customary sign at the corner letting visitors know that they were now entering a block where there were proud members of the Block Club who cared about the neighborhood's safety and appearance. Block clubs sort of remind me of Hansberry's *A Raisin in the Sun*, when the guy comes to visit the Younger family and he says he is from the Clybourn Park Improvement Association representing the neighborhood where the Youngers are all set to move. It creates more pride in your neighborhood when the entire block is vested in its upkeep and welfare. Don't get me wrong, it is not like there aren't any block clubs and block parties now. I see the block club signs as I travel throughout the city. It always makes my mind wander back to the days of my youth, when the families on the block worked together for the good of the block—whether it was during election time, campaigning, and voting, or buying nice, coordinated outdoor lights to be placed in front of the homes.

Our block was a two-way street for many years, and then it was changed into one way. After the new Seventh District Police Station was erected on the corner of Sixty-Third Street, the block was again opened up to traffic going in both directions.

When we weren't dancing during the block parties we were dancing inside the house to a variety of Motown music or Atlantic Records' musicians—from Dick Clark's American Bandstand to Don Cornelius' Soul Train and even Friday nights when we gathered around the small black and white television to watch Big Bill Hill. No matter the occasion, we all mugged and profiled before "vogueing" was in vogue. We imitated the people on television and tried to do the dances that we saw kids do who looked just like us. We were always fascinated by the black performers who would sometimes appear on the syndicated shows. My father would often ask, "Hey Elaine, can you do that dance?" Well, of course, I could do that dance or just pretended to do the jerk, the swim, or the boogaloo with the best of them.

The record-breaking homespun dance show Soul Train served as an inspiration to many black youth growing up in Chicago in the early 1970s. Cornelius with his big, thick afro was the man, as far as we were concerned. Many youth went downtown to Channel 26 to be on the show that he started with Clinton Ghent. Soul Train, as its name implied, showcased soul singers of the day, some well known and others not. The music that we gravitated to during that time was primarily dance music, and if you weren't downtown performing on the show, you were at home not only dancing to the music but also checking out the latest clothing styles, i.e., bell bottoms and platform shoes. These styles were also imitated throughout the South Side. Even though I took clothing and home economics classes at Gage Park, I couldn't stitch two seams together to save my life. However, I was always looking for ways to accentuate my meager wardrobe. While at Gage Park, I would constantly beg my brother to let me wear his Italian knit sweaters. "No, you will push out the top of the sweater," he would say, referring to whatever little knobs that I had that could pass for breasts.

Audrey could sew her butt off. She even made her own wedding dress. She would make nice dresses to wear to Lindblom High School; sometimes little mini dresses with a longer jacket to wear over it. She had an afro that topped off her look and she just left me in the wind when it came to styling and profiling. I could just pray that she would make me an outfit, too, or let me wear something that she had made for herself. Audrey and I were a long way from dressing alike, as we had done when we were younger. But Audrey had her own reasons for making her own clothes. "In high school, I always thought that I did not look good in pants, and I probably wanted to show off my big legs by wearing dresses all the time," she said. "Can you see me now in wood shop class in a dress with sawdust all over me?" We never had designer clothes and there really wasn't an emphasis on designer clothes during the late 1960s and early 1970s. Audrey, however, always wanted more. "I learned how to sew and after mastering the sewing machine, I made every type of dashiki you could imagine," she said. "I had the big afro, and hoop earrings at times, which was the standard look of the times." It was a good thing that Audrey was able to sew because there was another "Warden" rule in our home. We couldn't wear anybody else's clothes, meaning that we couldn't sneak out of the house to go to school and then go to a friend's home and switch clothes with her—but that happened anyway.

Audrey was so cool that she even smoked Virginia Slims cigarettes at one time. "I learned to smoke behind the garage, one sunny afternoon, but that was short lived because a neighbor called out to R.D. and told him that the garage was on fire," Audrey said. "Later on, the garage wasn't on fire, but my butt was. This was a true case of 'do as I say, not as I do'." She also agreed that, "Dad was strict, but it was best and we came out okay."

Audrey worked at Selfix, a company that made bathroom hooks and self-adhesive products. She even took the train at night back home and also worked at the Field Museum. Back then, it was safe coming home at night on public transportation.

These were cool things; to work at the Field Museum and tailor her own clothes. And she also got "big sister" points because she was into Bruce Lee movies. What a strange happenstance, but she loved Bruce Lee and James Milton "Jim" "the Dragon" Kelly. Their block buster movie "Enter the Dragon" was released in July of 1973, and I remember my sister not being content until she was able to see it.

Just as we couldn't wear a friend's clothing growing up, we also could not eat at anyone's house without permission, which was on rare occasion. One of Olivia's best friends was T.P. She was one of our neighbors who went to the local Catholic school. Her mother cooked every evening and dinner was ready for the entire family by 6 p.m. Sometimes when they were down the street at T.P's house, Olivia says that she and Phyllis would often get caught up in the essence of that family's dinner. "I could smell the aroma of chicken, rice and home-made gravy ('hmmmm), and I can almost smell it now," Olivia said. This should have been their cue to come home, but T.P.'s father, who was a police officer, would often ask them to stay. Every once in a while, if they caught my father just at the right moment, they would call home and he would allow them to stay over for dinner. And this was one of those times. For some reason, the chicken and gravy at a neighbor's house smelled better than it did at home. Maybe it was because there were only two kids taking in the aroma as opposed to five kids at our house! Once my sisters received permission to stay over, their eyes grew big, as the chicken with dripping gravy was piled onto their plates and even bigger when the seasoned, fluffy rice landed in its rightful place next to the chicken. Topped off with Kool-aid they couldn't go wrong! I know you are thinking that my sisters didn't appreciate meals at our home but to eat at a table where there may possibly be leftovers couldn't be all bad.

I was welcomed into my friend's house, just southeast of Englewood, on the city's "urban" side.

His father, answering the door, and his mother, in the kitchen, tending to something delicious smelling.

I was reminded of simpler times, of normalcy in chaos.

Every house in the hood ain't hood, and every house in the hood ain't good.

So you can imagine my calm and pleasure seeing this family representing our community,

and it was right, by sight.

Who knows what goes down behind closed doors?

But when you open your home, you open your vibe.

Inviting my world to intertwine.

As I said my hellos and goodbyes, my friend and I went to Englewood, on my side of town and filmed until the hood came around.

My grandmother, warning us to wrap it up, because we're not from around there, and not looking for trouble.

And at this time I'm seeing double.

When I was a child this same stoop was safe.

And now I'm reminded of a colder place.

But still, on that corner on Bishop, I feel the love resonating from simpler days.

And I thank my grandparents for that!

-----Psalm One

Fourteen

Plaits, Pressing Combs, Afros, Perms, Wave Nouveaus, and Dreadlocks

ost Saturday nights were reserved for getting our hair "hot combed or straightened" in preparation for church on Sunday. After a good wash and a bit of Hair Rep, Dixie Peach or Royal Crown, we would be set and ready to tie our hair down with a scarf, so we would look pretty on Sunday mornings. It was an arduous task. The nape of the neck, which is referred to as the "kitchen," always seemed to need a little extra grease and sizzle from the hot comb, which is kept hot on the eye of the stove. For those readers who don't know, a hot comb or straightening comb is a metal comb used to straighten or make "silky and soft" moderate or coarse hair that was the crowning glory of many young girls. The comb was heated on the stove and then ran through sections of hair, until the entire head of hair was nice, shiny and straight. My mother had to have a steady hand, and I had to have an even firmer hand as she worked around the ear. I had to hold my ear in a curled down position away from my head, lest she would burn my ear with the hot comb. A slip up was always possible and it was made evident by the dark, black burns left on the side of your face or ear. Sarah Breedlove, known by most as Madame C. J. Walker, is to be commended for improving this entire process and she is recognized as the first female self-made millionaire for doing so.

However, throughout the week, my mother would plait my hair in one plait with the entire head of hair going to the back and the little pig tail situated at the center. It wasn't enough for a long braid. But for Sunday and for special occasions, like a school assembly or something, our hair would be hot combed.

When I was older, probably in high school, I received my first perm, at Sarah's Beauty Shop, which was located near Sixty-Third Street and Loomis. I would sit there for what seemed like hours, until it was my time to get my hair sectioned off again. But this time a cold, smelly, white gook substance was applied to my head and left there until I couldn't stand the stinging heat any more. I didn't have to hold my own ears this time, because Sarah put a plastic cape around my body. She also lined my neck with sterile white wraps, so that my neck wouldn't burn if some of the perm fell off my head, as it was prone to do. Sure, go ahead—think Denzel Washington in *Malcolm X* when he just couldn't stand it any more while getting his first conk. If you recall this scene, my experience wasn't exactly as Malcolm's, but the longer I could stand for this lye substance to be in my hair the straighter my hair would get. Where oh where was soul singer "sistuh of the universe" India.Arie when I needed her?

Phyllis and Olivia were often each other's partners in crime when it came to hair, also. Phyllis grew up to have beautiful thick, flowing hair, but as much as it was thick, it was that much nappier and harder to comb. Many times when my mother was at work and Phyllis and Olivia were preparing to go to school, Olivia combed Phyllis' hair. "It hurt me as much as it hurt her," Olivia said. "Her hair was nappppyyyyy!" This grooming process was made all the more difficult because Phyllis hated with a passion to get up for school. But this disdain for early morning hours didn't give her a pass. None of us could just pretend to be sick and not attend school, simply because we couldn't pry ourselves away from the television the night before. Eventually, it became easier for Phyllis to catch the early morning rays. Nowadays Phyllis doesn't have to commit so much time to grooming her hair in the morning. As she grew older and moved to the East Coast, she abandoned her perms, and she now wears a short, short cut. Yep, no weave for her!

After a couple of decades or so of surviving the plait, the pressing comb and then the afro, perm, jheri curl, and wave nouveaus, I chose a short, faded cut in 1990. I sported a short, shaped afro in 1996 and then settled on twists and then official dreadlocks in 2000.

This is how I stumbled into a short haircut, after having travelled to the East Coast a few times and falling in love with all things Afro-centric. On the evening of September 21, 1990, I found myself surrounded by clippers, combs, solvents, and sterile, white neck wraps, all the accouterments of masculine hair grooming. What had led me to this place? In the 1970s I was much too European in my projections to even fleetingly consider such a notion. Well times had changed. Expensive trips to the beauty salons, the inability to maintain cornrows, or just the desire to express myself in a "politically-correct, Afro-centric" manner thrust me into this hirsute den.

Amid incredulous stares, I waited in the anteroom of Lou's Barber Shop on East Seventy-First Street in South Shore. The glances from the bruthas who were also waiting made me even more nervous about this ritual. I suppose they were trying to discern the relationship that I and my female companion, who was a co-worker, shared. One of the barbers did inquire as to whether or not I preferred to see a hair stylist on the other side of the room. "I want to get my hair cut," was my reply. He assured me that someone would be with me momentarily.

One brutha even asked me if my boyfriend would like me with short hair, another stab at trying to figure out my sexuality. "My boyfriend lives in New York and is a light-weight Malcolm X clone," I said. In other words, mind your own business.

Before long, a young man named J. arrived. J. was a pudgy, fat-cheeked lad who appeared to have just survived puberty and was as apprehensive about this whole ordeal as I. J., whom I assumed was a master barber, fingered my hair that was not as coarse as he was accustomed to and asked, "Just what do you want done?" I fumed a second, wondering if he asked this of all his customers. "Just cut it," I said sharply, pointing to the card displaying various haircuts. After agreeing upon a style, he started cutting. Thick, black tresses fell before my eyes. Nervous flitters filled my stomach. "How does it look?" I asked my friend. Her answer did not alleviate my fears. Nearly thirty short minutes later, with very short hair, I emerged from the shop, a new woman in search of large earrings.

It took me a while to find a permanent barber, and I found him at Grant's on East Eighty-Seventh Street in Chatham. He was older and more experienced. "Is your name Lorraine or Elaine," he would often ask me. Aside from combs, razors, and mirrors, Grant's was often filled with *Sports Illustrated* and *Time* magazines, and older, gray-haired men swapping stories of past conquests and current events.

"Here comes Mr. Money-bags," is how Grant used to greet his male clientele. Once in a while another woman would come in and I would feel more at home. I kept this faded cut for a few years, before eventually going to twists and dreadlocks. I never yearned for that wave noveau of the past, and I will always hold soft spots in my head and heart for J.

At the end of the day, I believe that as long as your hair is clean and in some neat fashion, it is fine no matter what chemical, or not, you have in it. And for those sistuhs who would rather buy their hair, that's fine, also. As a male physical education teacher once told me in grammar school, "As long as a girl has her hair in shape, it doesn't matter what she is wearing, as hair is a woman's crown."

Good hair is a gift.

Good hair is a curse.

Good hair is and isn't a woman's worth.

In college a "frienemy" cut my hair off, and my mother told me I was finally a boy.

Those words cut like a knife, and hurt more than that girl sabotaging the rest of my school year.

It was foul play, and that girl was never heard from again.

In time, both wounds healed, and I was able to rock my short perm with much confidence.

And in my new rocker sense, I still have this hair issue.

What hair issue?

To be natural or not?

To shave or to conk?

To weave or to wig?

To let live or to be hid?

I love my hair:

Thick as cement and as beautifully stubborn as it wants,

It has a life of its own that it flaunts.

God given, with strands of strength.

If I want it to be straight? Then hurry up and wait.

Black hair has been a grand discussion for centuries, and sometimes they love it more than what we see in we.

But I am here to tell you all, my mother's hair is stronger than ever when she let it be naturally strong.

She let her hair be as strong as she is, and through the plaits, jheri curls and fades, her mane is most beautiful now.

How fascinating it is when full circles come around.

-----Psalm One

Fifteen

Jones Commercial, My First Job, and a Whole New World Outside of Englewood

The opportunity to travel downtown for school was exciting. My siblings and I, however, had already had the experience of going downtown on numerous occasions. My mother would take us to places like Old Town and Buckingham Fountain, so I wasn't freaked out by this new area. It was a great experience to meet students from all across the city, as Jones was a selective school with admissions testing. I had good times at Jones. I was a good student and even served as Junior Class Secretary. I had friends not only from the South Side but from the West Side as well, which really helped me learn the city more, as we travelled the "EL" to each other's homes. There were students from other ethnicities with whom I became acquainted. One of my best buddies was my oldest friend Patricia, who lived just a couple of blocks east of me. She and I first met when we were around 10 years old, and we have been good friends since then. We attended grade school together and she and her sister both attended Jones. Most mornings, we would travel to school together and when we started working, we would often plan our after-work schedules to meet up again to travel back home. When I look back on those times, in hindsight, it was nice to get to know students from across the city and, as well, to be able to go downtown to school and get to travel outside of my comfort zone; to see just what made the "City of Big Shoulders" tick.

At Jones I learned how to operate a number of office machines, as well as learned typing and Gregg shorthand. I also learned how to run gigantic mimeograph machines that used a black film to make multiple copies. Another piece of office equipment that I mastered at Jones was the PBX (private branch exchange) telephone switchboard system, like the one you see in old movies or in the Lily Tomlin comedy routine. We also had to take grooming, because certainly young girls needed to be told how to walk and carry themselves around business people. "Walk straight and don't slouch," Ms. Hines would caution as I walked around the room with a book on my head. Olivia followed me and also graduated from Jones.

My first venture into the workforce in 1972 was as a secretary for the City of Chicago, Department of Water and Sewers. I was offered this job during my senior year at Jones, as all seniors had to work a half day. I originally started out at a job at the Loyola Law School Library on East Pearson Street, not far from Chicago's Magnificent Mile, but I complained after having gone to work in dresses (which was the attire for girls at Jones back then) and coming home on the "A" train to Ashland Avenue all dirty. My job consisted of changing the cardboard jackets glued to the front of each book, and those shelves and books were full of dust! I went to see Ms. Reed, who was a counselor at Jones. My skills were so good that she arranged for an interview with the City, which basically included myself and a few others sitting across a table chatting. A few days later, I was offered a job as a clerk in Administrative and Fiscal Services. Then after I graduated, I took the civil service test to become a stenographer. My job involved working with the accounting department, typing huge spreadsheets that weren't called spreadsheets at the time. And I certainly wasn't typing these reports on a computer. I used a manual typewriter with a wide carriage. When I made a mistake, I would just cut and paste that portion and replace it with the correct figures. The IBM Selectric typewriters, which seemed slick at the time with the "element" that you would swipe out in order to change the font, were used for other projects.

Once I started working for the City, my father helped me in the only way that he knew how. It was normally my mother to whom we went for advice, sometimes to just talk things out. But I remember before I started my job at City Hall, he told me to say "yes ma'am" and "yes sir," when I was addressing the white people downtown. When my father advised me to show deference to the white people with whom I would come into contact at my first job, the first thing that he was referring to was that old Southern, colored idea of inferiority that he believed I should consider when dealing with white people. It wasn't necessarily the idea that these people would be my boss and that I should defer to them because they held positions of authority. In that moment, it struck me that no matter how cute or smart I thought I was, wearing my nice little dresses and stockings and shoes, plopping on a nice hat and pulling on gloves, my father thought that I still had to make sure I kept my place and didn't disrespect the white people downtown. Heck, I didn't even have to say "yes ma'am and yes sir" to my parents. While I learned the ins and outs of working downtown, especially in City Hall, which was quite different than working at a bank or at an insurance company, I was the one who would shine, regardless, because I knew my stuff. Perhaps, it was at once a nod to my skills or a way of just using me, because I trained a few young white girls coming through the doors at City Hall. This need to be as good at my job as possible is still with me today. At times, I regret not necessarily perfecting or advancing my craft (whatever it happened to be at the moment) but I more so regret not asserting myself more when I felt encroached upon in the workplace.

The same way that I described getting a job in little or no time at the law firm was echoed when I first moved to Cincinnati. The firm was Honeywell. Even though I didn't accept the position, the attitude in 1978 of the white employers in regard to my skill set, knowledge, and professionalism seemed off-putting. I recall going to apply for a secretarial position and taking the standard shorthand and typing aptitude tests and the administrator being amazed at my test results. It was as if they wanted to make me take the tests over so they could see the "real" results. But those were the real results. Didn't these people know that my relatives in Chicago were proud of me and they thought that I ran the bank? So didn't they get the email that I was fully prepared? But no, these people were looking at my skin color and were hesitant.

I once even studied court stenography and didn't complete the certificate because of some earth-shattering "oh my goodness" need to switch gears and do something else. Whenever I see a court stenographer I think of the classes and the machine and the fleeting key strokes that created "ladies and gentlemen of the jury." Recently I was waiting on the "EL" and across the railing behind me I could see into the windows of MacCormac College. I could see students there who could have easily been in my age bracket studying and "key stroking" away. Even though this isn't the college I attended, it took my mind back to "what if?"

The comings and goings at City Hall were something to behold for a 16-year-old girl from the South Side. Powerbrokers would come through the hallways, dressed in nice suits, ties, leather loafers and pinky rings, while carrying leather briefcases. They would go for lunch at restaurants with such names as Mayor's Row, Hinkey Dink's Tavern and Counselor's Row. This scene made for some eye popping circumstances, while walking through that great and distinguished building. You didn't have to know that there may have been some unscrupulous dealings going on; it was just a marvel to behold the constant activity.

I was working at the City when the first Mayor Daley passed away in December 1976. Mayor Richard J. Daley had ruled the city for twenty-one years and afterward his body would lie in state in the hallways of the building that he had known so well. His son Richard M. Daley served as Chicago's mayor from 1989 until 2011, when he decided not to run again. But before the son came into office, Chicago witnessed the election of its first African American mayor, Harold "you want Harold, you got him" Washington. Washington ran a successful grass-roots campaign and was adored by the masses. He was first elected in April 1983 and won re-election in 1987. Unfortunately, he died in office in November 1987. His personality was infectious, and the city mourned his passing. It left many African Americans wondering just when we would see another black mayor. We weren't even thinking at the time that we would see something more profound than another black mayor. We would live to see Pres. Obama elected to the highest office in our nation—not once but two times.

Hanging out with my co-workers during this time meant discovering the upscale Marshall Field & Company (Macy's), after I had been used to buying dresses and clothes at Lerner Shops and other stores in the downtown area. An older co-worker taught me about buying quality instead of quantity; therefore, Marshall Field's seemed like the best choice. It wasn't cheap and there weren't many black salespeople working there at the time. As a matter of fact, at one time, Field's had a history of not being too welcoming to minorities, but I was too young to even realize or get involved in political correctness by boycotting the store.

I also learned about the Millionaire's Club where you could get a good meal or a Sloe Gin Fizz or Tom Collins. We swore that they must have been mixing those drinks in the bathtub because you got free drinks with your meals. But they were not that strong. I ate my first lobster there, some time in my senior year of high school and brought the shell home for a souvenir. After having it in the dresser drawer for about a week, it started stinking and my mother wondered just what it was. I didn't toss it; however, I just went down to the basement and washed it clean in the washtub. I also discovered a club on West Eighty-Seventh

Street in Gresham that is still there now, Reese's. It wasn't a matter of trying to be grown; it was more a situation where I was young and working with a slightly older crew, and lunch time and events right after work exposed me to what were then considered the finer or more exciting things in life.

There was a man who preached with a bull horn and small amplifier: "You can't get to Heaven smoking that reefer," he admonished passersby. "And those of you who are living in sin won't get to Heaven, either," he proclaimed. I would see this man on the streets of downtown Chicago preaching the Gospel in the early 1970s and he is still there today. My buddies and I would also sometimes go to Flo's, Beef and Brandy, and The Court to eat meals. All located downtown, these places welcomed the younger crowd, especially those who had money to pay for their meals. Flo's made the best malts around, and there was also the Little Heidelberg, Ronny's Steak House, which is still in business, and 'Round the Clock restaurants. The Court had a disco that was very popular well into the 1980s. The place would be packed on Friday nights with an urban, professional crowd, looking for good, clean fun, food and what seemed like endless dancing.

It was so cool to be downtown working. It made me feel more mature and it certainly helped my parents since I had my own money. This first job served as my training ground, but sadly it opened my eyes to the discrimination that prevailed in Chicago. One of the disconcerting aspects about working for the City at that time was that many of my co-workers were from Bridgeport, a neighborhood made famous in one respect because the Daley family, which produced two Chicago mayors, came from that area. Another outstanding reference to Bridgeport came later in 1997 with the well-publicized beating of 13-year-old Lenard Clark, a black teen who lived in a nearby housing project, by a group of young white youth in an area bordering Bridgeport. He was just riding his bike in the neighborhood after playing basketball and was targeted and kicked into a coma that resulted in brain damage. Newspaper reports of the ensuing trial were graphic in nature and recounted sentiments from across the nation. An *Associated Press* article about the trial, written by Mike Robinson on April 19, 1998 and titled *Trial to put racism in spotlight*, began this way:

When Lenard Clark was found crumpled and unconscious on a South Side street, the victim of a brutal beating, police had no doubt about the motive. The black 13-year-old had bicycled into a mostly white neighborhood one night last spring, and the color of his skin apparently sparked an attack so violent it touched a nerve across the nation.

President Clinton asked Americans to pray for the youngster left comatose by a 'savage and senseless assault driven by nothing but hate.'

Thirteen months later, the three young white men charged with trying to kill Lenard Clark are about to go on trial in a case that dramatically underscores the nation's unresolved racial tensions. The scene of the beating, Armour Square, is at the edge of Bridgeport, a neighborhood of tidy blue-collar homes that has given Chicago four mayors in 50 years—two of them named Daley.

When I was working and had associates from Bridgeport, that area was off limits to blacks. A co-worker having a baby shower was told by her landlord that he better not ever see her inviting niggers to her apartment or he would evict her. She was very apologetic and I just brushed it off, pretending or masking that I didn't want to go anyway. Here we were nearly twenty-five years later and racism was still prevalent in that neighborhood.

Something else that I noticed was that there appeared to be much patronage and nepotism going on; with many relatives working in the same city departments. If you worked the pavement and solicited votes at the request of the local committeeman, you were guaranteed a job. This "good ol' boys club" would later be dismantled by a 1983 court order called the Shakman decree that made it unlawful to take any political factor into account in hiring public employees.

Today, Bridgeport is more integrated, and I live only about a mile or so east of there. But I can't seem to get over my past experiences with residents of that area who seemed so vehemently against integration. They welcomed the Asian community as residents, but this was probably because they primarily spoke their own language, so the native Bridgeporters could still feel slightly superior. But the area has definitely changed, with many Latinos and blacks now living there.

Proud, dignified 1973 Jones graduate

Sixteen

Club Hopping and Greasy Spoons

B y the time I had graduated I wasn't quite 17, but that didn't stop me from following Audrey to clubs on the South Side; namely, Bernard's Place, Mr. Rickey's Chic Rick House, the Green Bunny, Bonanza, the High Chaparral, the Fantasy, Sheba Disco, the Packing House, East of the Ryan, the Roadrunner, the Copherbox, Dingbats to see Doc's Bad Boys, the Burning Spear, and the Ridgeland, among others. I can hear Donna Summer's *Love to Love You Baby* playing at the Ridgeland, on a week night to boot, and the smoke machine creating an atmosphere that kept us dancing all night. In those days, before either of us had automobiles, we used public transportation to get from place to place, or we bummed rides from people. "It must be White Castle if it's 2 a.m." was a familiar refrain, because we always seemed to end up at that fast food joint famous for sliders (small burgers with grilled onions) or at a bar-be-que joint on Halsted after a night out on the town.

For a couple of years, however, we begged our father to let us travel by Metra train to Southern Illinois University, where the Kappa Karnival was being held. We went down to Carbondale, Illinois, not really having a clue as to what we were in for. We just knew it was a trendy thing to do at the time, and many of our contemporaries went also. One year I ran into an old boyfriend of mine, a guy I had met after following my sister to a party a few years earlier. This party was on the South Side, near Sixtieth Street and Green, and O.G. and I met and sort of danced the night away. Of course, when my sister was ready to go, I wasn't quite ready, but she dragged me home anyway. We were responsible for each other; we didn't go out together and NOT return home together. The next day after church, O.G. came by to meet my parents and ask my father if I could go to see *The Godfather*. It wasn't No. 1 or No. 2 at that time. It was just the first one. Naturally, we took the train downtown and had a good time. It was keeping in line with the whole "movies after church theme."

O.G. had that famous "black man walk" about him and he was a proud brutha, very respectful but really, really cool. You know how comedians describe Pres. Obama's walk. It's a walk that cannot be ignored. When a brutha walks that way, you know he is either going somewhere or he's been somewhere important! We dated after that and through the summer, but he had warned me that once September came and school started, we wouldn't see much of each other because he had to play football at his high school. He escorted me to a couple of dances at Jones through the fall and the following spring, and that was about it. He would show up at my home in nice suits. He once had a long coat that had a "Sherlock Holmes" cape. We would happily get on the "A" train and go downtown to Jones to show off. At Jones, since there were more female than male students, when parties and events occurred, it always seemed like a game or competition to see just what kind of guys the female students were dating. When we both graduated O.G. went away to Lane College in Jackson, Tennessee, so it was nice seeing him in Carbondale.

This is what weekend entertainment amounted to during the time directly after high school. Since my sister and I graduated from high school together because I skipped a grade, we sort of followed each other around, hanging out with each other's friends across town. And when she finally bought a car, it was time to spread out to the Machine on the North Side and other clubs, packing as many friends into the car as possible.

One particularly memorable moment was when my girlfriend Regina and I took a photo with Chicago's Chi-Lites, in the summer of 1975. After their performance at either the High Chapperal or the Burning Spear, we were able to get a photo with them. I still have that photo, with me in pink linen slacks, a pink printed blouse with a tank underneath, a pink and white Totes waterproof scarf that I bought downtown from Carson, Pirie, Scott and Co., all while holding a straw hat and umbrella.

From time to time, as young teens we would get some adult to take us to the Regal Theater on East Forty-Seventh Street to see the reigning black act of the day. Another one of my father's children, an older sister named Gloria Jean, would visit us in the summer. She took us to see James Brown, and all I remember about that day was the screaming. I couldn't understand then what it was all about, even though I do now. The Chicago International Amphitheatre near Forty-Second Street and South Halsted, where the Chicago Auto Show was once held, was also a popular venue in the early- to mid-1970s. My two younger sisters were privileged to see the Jackson Five there, after much prodding and arranging with neighbors and chaperones. My other recollection of the Amphitheatre was when our Uncle Johnnie took us to see the Ringling Brothers and Barnum & Bailey Circus. He would take us early enough to stop at the greasy spoon right near the venue, and then we went inside to see all the animals. There were horses and tigers and other animals, but the elephants were always my favorite, even though I wouldn't want to get too close to them. We also thought that Uncle Johnnie was so handsome, because he was a sharp dresser and kept a nicely manicured goatee. He also lived in our basement at one time or another and he was married to one of my cousins.

During all of those nights out, we never worried about issues of the day like crime, crossing gang territories, or things of that nature. It was just good, clean fun and socializing among teens and young adults when we went to the clubs.

Seventeen

My Father - Randolph

||||||||||||||||||||||||||||||||||||||||||||||||||||||||||||||||||||||||||||||||||||||||||||||||||||||||||||||

When we weren't going to the movies on Sundays, our other enjoyment was when my father would pack us all in the car and take us to the drive-in. He would pop a big bucket full of popcorn, and we would only have to buy pop or soda. There would be my parents and one of us in the front seat and the other four siblings would be seated in the back. We would roll the car window down, place the speaker inside of the car, and then roll the window back up to keep the speaker in place. My parents would stay in the car, and we would go to the concession stand to get pop and whatever else we could buy with our money. After he ate a bit of popcorn, drank some coffee, and smoked a cigarette, which to me didn't go together, my father would go to sleep until we woke him up after the movie was over. Going to the drive-in was a real treat since it was a family event where we all had fun.

My father was a smoker. He smoked more than a pack a day when we were kids. He smoked many different brands, but Viceroy is one that sticks out with me, as well as Kool Menthol 100's. There was a store called Whitelaw's located at the corner of Sixty-Second Street and Ada, not far from our home where as pre-teens we would go and buy my father cigarettes. At his direction, my mother or someone would just write a note and ask for the cigarettes, and Mr. Whitelaw who sat at the front of the store with all of his girth and dressed in a white t-shirt while examining the "numbers" sheet would oblige. No one paid attention to the Surgeon General's warning or the fact that pre-teens were actually buying cigarettes.

There was no public outcry about second-hand smoke. For one buck, you could get a pack of cigarettes and have more than enough change to buy potato chips and Now and Laters, banana splits, nut chews, Bit-O-Honey and an assortment of other penny candies. Oh, life was good!

The "numbers" sheet, as I remember, was a sheet with various combinations of numbers on it that was used for gambling. I considered it a precursor to the lottery since poor, black folks would place a bet with the local numbers runner and wait to see if their number hit, which meant there was some kind of payoff. I had never seen my parents fool with this game of chance but a neighbor across the street had her own enterprise. I just remembered that she kept strips upon strips of paper with numbers written on them in shoe boxes. Research reveals that the game was called "Policy," and bets were taken for as little as a penny. While this game may have been something that blacks from the Southern states transplanted up North, I remember West Indian Archie, played by Delroy Lindo in *Malcolm X*, as head of his own numbers racket. That research posits that my neighbor would have been known as a "policy queen" and she probably had someone, a "runner," who went and recorded the numbers that individuals wanted to bet; and conversely, paid out winnings to individuals who won.

Author Christine Fletcher writes in *Ten Cents A Dance* that the slips of paper were known as "policy slips" and that in Chicago this game, which started in the late 1800s, continued to be controlled by blacks in the city. "The policy racket was originally controlled by African-Americans, who became known as the policy kings (and queens—a few women ran numbers games, too)," she said. "But by the 1930s, white gangsters had taken over the racket in all major Northern cities except one—Chicago. In Chicago, the policy kings formed a syndicate that successfully fought off takeover by white organized crime for over 20 years. That kept control of the racket in the African-American community. And where the control was, so were the profits."

Another author Nathan Thompson writes in his acclaimed novel *Kings: The True Story of Chicago's Policy Kings and Numbers Racketeers, An Informal History* that "Policy became the biggest black-owned business in the world with combined annual sales sometimes reaching the $100 million mark and employing tens-of-thousands of people nationwide. In Bronzeville [a South Side Chicago neighborhood], Policy was a major catalyst by which the black economy was driven. In 1938, *Time* magazine reported that Bronzeville was the 'Center of U.S. Negro Business,' and more than a decade later, *Our World* magazine reported that 'Windy City Negroes' have more money, bigger cars and brighter clothes than any other city....The city which has become famous for the biggest Policy wheels, the largest funerals, the flashiest cars and the prettiest women, has built that reputation on one thing, money." Thompson writes that these attributions were largely due to Policy, "a business conceived, owned, and operated by African-American men known by many names....but more often than not they were called 'Policy Kings.' "

However, in 1974, a little game called the Illinois State Lottery came into existence. Afterward, nobody had to hide their affinity for gambling since it was now legal—all in the name of primarily supporting public school education.

As I mentioned, I never saw my father play the numbers because he had to keep all the money that he had to support his family and buy his cigarettes. When he wanted a larger quantity of cigarettes than we could buy at Mr. Whitelaw's and needed a little gas also, he would pack a few of us up and drive far southeast to the "last liquor store," which was located in Indiana. Though it was probably located just at the end of the Skyway it sure seemed much farther away. But it wasn't really that far because Indiana and Illinois border each other. Once we got there, we would buy candy, my father would get his cigarettes, and we were set for awhile. I was in the store recently and a man purchased two packs of cigarettes for a total of more than $26. Cigarette taxes in Chicago are crazy, but the increased cost still doesn't seem to be enough to prevent people from buying them. Can you imagine just what that $26 could have purchased decades ago?

My mother and father would go out from time to time. My father had co-workers who lived in the south suburbs, and we had uncles who lived in areas on the South and West sides of the city. Whenever my parents went out the conversation went like this: "If you guys are good we will bring you something back." And naturally, they would always bring us something back. Many times it would be bar-be-que ribs from the Painted Doll, which was located on West Fifty-Ninth Street near Halsted, or just some hamburgers. Of course we would try to wait up for the goodies.

Sometimes my father would dress up on Friday. After returning home from work, taking a bath with Tide washing detergent, shaving with Blue Magic shaving powder, and splashing on a bit of cologne; he would go to his "union" meeting. Now I don't really know if my father was in a union or not. I never recalled any propaganda literature around the house or any word about some political "uprising" rallying for better working conditions. But when my father dressed up to go to his "union" meeting on Friday night he would be dressed to the "nines" and "clean as the Board of Health." And you believed that there was a movement afoot! He would usually wear a suit with a shirt. Sometimes the suit would be a light plaid and the shirt could very well be a soft stripe, but the colors would match. "My father would smell so good when he went to the union meetings," said my sister Audrey. He would have on his gigantic gold chain with a cross on it. This was pre-Hip-Hop era, so he wasn't rocking the chain like Flavor Flav and his gold clock. My father would also have on a wool hat or a nice straw hat if it was during the warmer months, as men wouldn't be considered dressed without the customary hat.

Most men of that time, if they had worked hard all week and had a penchant for going out and having a good time, brought with them through the door a certain swagger (to use a contemporary word). My father had his certain swagger, also. Of course the cigarette would be ever present. I really don't know how my father got dressed nor did many things because he always seemed to have a cigarette in his mouth. Sometimes it would dangle from his mouth if he was busy with his hands. I would watch it burn away, with ashes falling down, looking as if the fire would burn his mouth. He would go out, have his fun at the union meeting, pay his dues, possibly have a couple of drinks, and return home. He would stay long sometimes, and at times even longer. You know, just long enough to have been out but just slightly short enough to not get questioned by my mother. I have only rarely seen my father drink; ours wasn't the house where there was a bar filled with spirits. However, when we went to some of my relatives' homes there may have been liquor there. I would assume that my father did occasionally drink because when he passed away I found a couple of liquor bottles in a cabinet in the kitchen. But no one could say, "Oh, R.D. he drinks all the time."

But we just as well should have been sleeping when he came home because Saturday was not a day of leisure. It was a day of chores, and sometimes we girls would take care of paying the bills. A treat for us was going to Maxwell Street to Howard Style Shop to pay my father's clothing bill. I'm sure he bought any number of nicely tailored suits from Howard's, but the Dobbs hats came from another location. We would take the bus to Halsted and then north on Halsted to Roosevelt Road, or Twelfth Street.

We didn't do the grocery shopping. That was always left for my parents. I remember that when my parents went grocery shopping they sometimes went to my Uncle Eddie's grocery store. They would bring these big boxes home, and we would scoot in the boxes playing in the hallway between the dining room and the kitchen. My father would buy big five-gallon containers of ice cream, like the ones you see in the ice cream shops. He would place this and other meats in the deep freezer that every large family needed in order to save money and shop more efficiently. He insured that we didn't have to beg for ice cream when the Good Humor truck came by peddling to the neighborhood kids. But one time Olivia ran out to the truck, and in her excitement she almost got hit by a car. After that time, I don't think she cared if the Good Humor truck came by or not. There were other near misses like that. As we got older Audrey and Randy were more often responsible for us. When we were younger, my father would go off to work early in the morning and get home after 4 or 5 in the evening. I can recall that he would leave his work pants with change in the pockets on the floor, and we sometimes would sneak in the pockets and just grab change. We figured he was going to give it to us anyway.

One day having just a little change nearly got Phyllis either hit by a car or chastised by my father. Phyllis was about 12 years old when she was riding her bike down to the end of the block, across the street and down Sixty-Third Street to get candy from Big Mama's store. Big Mama was nice and round too, much like Mr. Whitelaw. Maybe those two were married or otherwise related. It's noteworthy that we called the neighborhood merchants by some endearing name, which made Englewood more like the village that it was. As Phyllis was managing the turn onto the street she was hit by a car. After the ambulance came and they arrived at Englewood Hospital, Phyllis had to give up her change so my mother could call home. Though Phyllis still had her candy money in her pocket, she had more tears in her eyes. Not because of the pain, as she was only slightly hurt and recovered quickly. She was more concerned about my father whipping her for riding the bike across the street. But she was spared any punishment. The visit to the hospital was punishment enough. My father was too tired to whip her anyway. It was the early evening, and he probably was busy having another cigarette before watching a bit of television and retiring for the night.

Eighteen

My Mother - Ms. Pinkie

||||||||||||||||||||||||||||||||||||||||||||||||||||||||||||||||||||||||||||||||||||||||||||||||||||||||||||||||||||||

My mother's name is Pinkie, and she was born in 1933 in Shaw, Mississippi. Her mother's name was Laura. My mother didn't know her mother well because of the circumstances of her birth. To this day, my mother doesn't have a birth certificate, but this isn't unusual for folks born in the South. You see, my maternal grandmother was a cook working in Mississippi when she became pregnant with my mother. Back then, she was obligated to work for and have sexual relations with the white boss; and in 1933 when my mother was born, she appeared to be darker skinned than the siblings born before her. Even though fair-skinned (from where she got her name), she had actually taken on the darker color of my grandmother. The white boss was so upset thinking that my grandmother had slept with the stable hand that my grandmother sent my mother away to a neighbor woman and later on to Memphis to live with a relative. "My Uncle Emmett came to Mississippi to get me, and I lived with him in Memphis until I was in the eighth grade," my mother said. "During the summers, I came back to Mississippi, but it was a long while before I knew who my mother actually was."

Uncle Emmett would send my mother money to Mississippi to make sure that she didn't need anything. "Uncle Emmett showed me a life in Memphis that I wouldn't have had in Mississippi," my mother said. "Not only did Uncle Emmett shower me with love, affection, and material things, my brother Eddie would also come to Memphis during those years and bring me riding boots and jodhpurs and take me horseback riding."

Uncle Eddie was a Pullman Porter, and throughout my mother's life he always wanted better for her. "He encouraged me later in life to go to school to be a stenographer because I always wanted to work in an office but never did in the way that I had wanted," she said. My mother said that Uncle Eddie would take her out to dinner and admonish her if she wanted to order just a hamburger. "I suppose since he was a Pullman Porter he saw many, many things," my mother said, "Of course he would rather that I ordered a steak. He would also bring me fancy magazines, and I would dream of dressing and being just as beautiful as the white women that I saw on the pages."

My mother recalled a time in Memphis when she was about 13 years old and in the eighth grade. "I have never been in a classroom with white students and I excelled in English and reading," my mother said. "I was just that good and I was exempt from taking some of the department exams." One Christmas the teacher gave gifts to the students. My mother said that while she was excited about the holiday, she was slightly disappointed in her teacher. "She was giving out gifts, and I thought that I would get perfume or some jewelry, and she gave me a book." And it wasn't just that she gave my mother a book, it was the subject of the book; Mein Kampf, loosely an autobiography of German dictator Adolf Hitler. "I appreciated that my teacher thought that I was well advanced, but that book was so difficult to read that I never really got into it." After hearing this story I wondered just how a connection could even had been made between Hitler and a young, black girl from Mississippi.

A short time after this, my grandmother came to fetch my mother just out of the blue. "My mother had to go to court to get me," my mother said. "I don't know why all of a sudden she came to claim me, and I only returned to Mississippi for a short time before moving again with my Uncle Emmett to Gary, Indiana." My mother lived with Uncle Emmett near Twenty-Fifth Street and Grant. She attended Roosevelt High School for a couple of years, dropping out while in the tenth grade when math became too hard for her. Later, my mother returned to Mississippi because she said that she was beginning to be a handful for my Uncle Emmett and his wife, Lucinda. It was during this trip back to Mississippi that she married my father. She was not quite 16 and my father was 23. My mother said that she and my father had known each other through the years, because all the families in that part of Mississippi knew each other. I admit growing up that it wasn't a "Claire and Cliff" family environment all the time. But my parents and our family stuck together as most families of the day managed to do. My mother would eventually know her siblings; but we never knew my maternal grandmother, although we did know my aunts and uncles on my mother's side. As a matter of fact, one of my mother's sisters and her children actually lived with us in our home at one time.

During the early part of her marriage, my mother owed much to her brothers Bobby and Eddie and her Uncle Emmett because she said they did a lot for her. "Even when R.D. and I were married and living in Chicago, Bobby would send me money just because he wanted to make sure that we were not struggling," she said. "Once he had sent me about $300 and I paid about $100 for some shoes. It seemed as much as that, although they may not have cost $100. R.D. and I went to Delores Photography on Forty-Seventh Street and State to take a nice photo." My mother says she doesn't remember exactly why they took the photo, but it was in 1953 while she was pregnant with my brother. "I suppose I wanted to document the event, but R.D. was furious that I had spent so much money for my shoes." I guess my mother was feeling good about herself and her pregnancy, so she wanted a fancy photo to look at years later—feeling like the Ms. Pinkie that she would affectionately be called by neighbors. It is a beautiful photo, and my mother had on a nice suit, with clutch purse in lap and hair nicely coiffed. My father had on a nice brown suit and hat atop his head. Though I don't profess to be in this bunch, many writers when discussing the Great Migration speak about when families reach their "New World" destination that they want to capture that moment in history, probably to send copies to folks back home. Even though my mother may have "sold the farm" to purchase her outfit, I am sure that her Uncle Emmett would have been proud to see her all decked out—looking as if she had long arrived in a town with many strangers. But these strangers were all from one united family, that of blacks "seeking a city."

My mother would help anybody with anything. She has a generous spirit and she is one of the last original members of Trinity Missionary Baptist Church. I would imagine that if there were only five members, my mother would still attend the church where she and my father sent all five children to get that old school religious upbringing. In the early 1960s, my mother worked at Garden City Laundry on South Plymouth Court in the South Loop. Chicago was once called the Garden City because of its motto: Urbs in Horto or City in a Garden. Later she worked in the laundry department at Rush Presbyterian St. Luke Hospital and then as a mail clerk at the famed Palmer House in downtown Chicago. She was working at the Palmer House during my years at Jones, and I enjoyed going down to visit her after school. Just walking through the majestic lobby of that hotel put me in a state of mind that had me travelling to faraway places. But my first stop would have been down the street to the old Goldblatt's store that seemed to sell everything in the basement. As you made your way up State Street, there were stores after stores in which a young high school senior could well find ways to spend her paycheck.

Downtown wasn't a place where young black kids went all the time, and Jones' students could easily be recognized because the girls wore hats and gloves, and the young men wore suits. At that time, Jones only had juniors and seniors. When it was time for me to start at Jones, I had to borrow gloves from my mother's best friend, who lived around the corner. She had plenty of white gloves because she was an usher at church. This same lady, along with her husband and young family, had also lived on Federal Street in the same apartment building with my family. Her name was Ms. Lessie. Our families all grew up in the church together. When I would drive my mother and Ms. Lessie somewhere to a church or social event, she would be so gracious for the ride. These two spirit-filled women would have a mini revival in the back seat. "Thanks, 'Laine' (is how Ms. Lessie would say my name), we thank God for this blessing of a ride." When they grew older and both of their husbands had passed away, Ms. Lessie and my mother became little activists in their own right. They would go downtown to tackle "The Man" in one city department after another. When she passed away my mother was really sad because they had been friends for at least fifty years. The Trinity family was sad, as well, because Ms. Lessie had been a neighborhood fixture.

In the late 1960s when the Black Power movement was strong, many street vendors would go door to door and sell their goods, i.e., brushes, socks, towels. One day a man came by the house selling whatever his particular item was, and he asked Audrey if my mother was home. He cautioned that he was only selling to blacks, and there were still whites living on our block. When the guy said he was only selling to black people, my sister told him, "Well, you don't need to talk to my mother because our mother is white." Now, she probably said this because my dear mother has fair skin. Despite the disconnect that my mother had from her birth mother, she had a good life growing up. Consequently, my mother wanted her children to have happy childhoods, as well. It was nothing for her to take us to the Riverview Amusement Park, which was a few long bus rides from our home. Riverview was a place where families went for entertainment in the late 1960s, blacks and whites, alike. I can't recall any instances of discrimination, but I was young. Years later, we were able to take the bus ourselves to a new amusement park called Fun Town, which was located closer to our home.

Growing up, along with her delectable peach cobbler, we enjoyed my mother's "tea cakes," which were sort of like thick sugar cookies. We would have the customary black eyed peas and corn bread, neck bones, greens with ham hocks or some other pig part to see us through the day. And the cornbread had crunchy corners and the top was nicely browned with delicate splits across. On Saturday nights we would help prepare whatever meal she was planning for Sunday dinner. During the week, my mother would sometimes start a meal early in the morning before she went to work and instruct us to start the pots up when we got home from school.

When we became sick with a cold, my mother would take a teaspoon full of sugar, add a couple of drops of kerosene, and hold the spoon over the flame for a couple of seconds. When it dissolved into the sugar and cooled off, we would drink it and this would dissipate the cold and phlegm in the chest. This is an old-time remedy that folks from the South used to cure the common cold. It didn't seem appealing at the time, especially for those who hated to drink the concoction. Why would anyone want to swallow kerosene—no matter how sweet tasting it had become? But this remedy soothed the worst colds during the worst winters for which Chicago is famous. Other times Father John's, cod liver oil, cocoa quinine or other medicines would do just fine for the kids. And being rubbed down at night on the chest with Vick's Vapor Rub was a nice, soothing treat for us when we were young, even though it seemed unbearable. There's a whole lot of love that has to go into a mother rubbing her child's chest down at night and carefully pulling the chenille bedspread over that child's body in that tiny twin bed—all in an effort to take one more step in keeping her children healthy.

Many times my mother would dress Audrey and me alike since we were a year apart. Phyllis and Olivia would also dress alike since they were a year apart and very close. Olivia says that because she skipped a grade and she and Phyllis ended up in the same grade, she felt that they sort of grew up as twins. Wherever Phyllis went, my mother almost always made her take Olivia with her, and Phyllis didn't like that responsibility all the time. She couldn't seem to shake her shadow. "We dressed alike often; and every other day, my mother would lay out our clothes on the couch for the next two days," Olivia said. "Yes, we wore our outfits two days in a row!"

Olivia excitedly recalled one sunny Mother's Day when the two of them had saved money and bought my mother greeting cards and a box of chocolate candy (Milk Duds). They were so proud of themselves but first had to argue over just which one of them would actually hand the yellow box over to my mother. "As our love grew bigger and our hearts expanded, that small box of candy seemed gigantic in our hands," Phyllis said. "It was surely large enough for us both to grasp and hand off to my mother together." And although hard to chew, my mother treated the Milk Duds as if she had received Godiva chocolates.

My brother was sort of on his own because he was the only boy, but he had male cousins and neighborhood friends with whom to keep company and have his own kind of fun. I recall that my brother was able to go to the annual Chicago Auto Show with his friend, Howard, and they would plan as soon as they found out just when all the nice, shiny automobiles and concept cars would be showcased at the International Amphitheatre. It was just magnificent because all kids dream about a nice new shiny car, well, especially the boys. It was hard for us girls to even try to get in on the mix. "I don't want to have to babysit at the auto show," my brother would say, as we begged to go. When he returned home late into the night, he would always have these nice, big, colorful car magazines.

After leaving the Palmer House, my mother worked as a switchboard operator at Rush Presbyterian St. Luke's Medical Center until her early retirement in 1989. She had switched jobs for better benefits. Certainly she now enjoys some of the best health care benefits available today through that retirement plan. This is a blessing and one less worry for our family.

However, after all these years, my mother has never learned how to drive because she had always been chauffeured by my father, which I believe was a common thing for many married women when we were growing up. There weren't that many "soccer" moms, pulling out the station wagon taking the brood to the park or to school; well at least not on our block. When we were younger I recall my mother going for a driving lesson with my father. He brought someone along with him, and as they both were trying to tell my mother how to stop, proceed or turn a corner, my mother unfortunately hit the gas pedal and a tree; and her eye was messed up for a while. Afterward, she never learned how to drive, but that doesn't stop her from getting anywhere that she needs to go.

Nineteen

Viceroy Cigarettes, Lung Cancer, and Death

A t one time Viceroy cigarettes were one of the least expensive cigarettes made, and my father smoked these, among other brands, for years. As a matter of fact, he smoked too many cigarettes during his lifetime.

Around July 4, 1986, my father had stopped smoking because he was coughing all the time. He slowed down doing anything extra around the house or even the garage. Seventeen days later he was admitted into the hospital. There is something really strange about that day because my father went to work in the south suburban town of South Holland and later that night we got a phone call from Rush Hospital (yes the same hospital where my mother worked as a switchboard operator) saying that my father had been admitted. My father had been in pain most of the day, and he bypassed our home and drove all the way to the near West Side to the emergency room. He was diagnosed, with the doctor telling us that they couldn't do anything and that the cancer had spread. He said that my father only had a few months to live. How does the doctor get to say how long someone has to live? The following day doctors did a biopsy and found a spot on his right lung. It was determined that the entire right lung was cancerous but no chemotherapy or surgery was scheduled. The cancer had spread throughout his blood system.

On July 29 my father came home from the hospital. "Mr. Hegwood, we advise you to do all the things that you have wanted to do," the doctor told my father. "Case studies with this type of cancer at this stage show that you have between three and four months to live."

My brother thinks that because my father had recently been to the dentist it created a way for the cancer to metastasize. So the next approximately sixteen days amounted to my father's demise. He would go back and forth to the hospital, and we welcomed family and friends who came over to see him. He would never go back to the basement apartment again. He had to sleep and be cared for upstairs. The next morning he seemed fine, coughing only slightly. He was taking milk of magnesia to correct his irregularity. He only had a prescription for Metamucil. "It's so ironic, I thought, you get the flu and the doctor gives you a prescription for Tylenol. But you're expiring from cancer and you get a prescription for Metamucil." It seemed that my father wanted privacy, as we were crowding him to some extent. Eventually, this overbearing wore off but we still didn't want to see him suffer any at all. Later that night, we could tell that he was in a lot of pain, but he wouldn't say how much. He took some Panadol pills that we were finally able to get, so I assumed he was uncomfortable. He got up from bed at least three times during the night and my mother was up all night. My siblings and I had started alternating days off to give my mother a break between her caretaking and going to work.

But I'm confused because my father isn't saying all the things that I think people should say when they know they are dying. Does he think he's invincible, or does he think he will have enough strength to be around next year? "Unless he gets deathly ill, there's no need bringing him into the hospital. It is tiring and he doesn't have too much longer," the doctor told my mother. As the days passed, the house seemed to be filled with visitors, and his eyes appeared to be sunken into his face.

My brother has come to cut my father's hair, and he looks so sad trying to be strong. Cristalle doesn't seem to know exactly what is going on.

She just knows that she hasn't been in the old Volkswagen van with my father for a while. The two used to go to McDonalds and get burgers, as well as to Lem's, the bar-be-que joint, to get ribs. Then, my father would sit up front, smoking cigarettes and watching the television that he had installed in the front of the van, while my poor kid was left to her own devices. But as long as those two were together, my father was happy. And as long as Cristalle had McDonald's she was deliriously happy.

Shortly after, my father had another doctor's appointment and my Uncle Archie came by to take him. Uncle Archie is the same brother that rented my family a place when my parents first came to Chicago. Around this time, my uncles were commenting on the fact that my father hadn't gone to the Veterans Administration Hospital. During the following days, my father would ingest Vick's Vapor Rub. "It is clearing me up," he insisted. You know, older people from down South think that Vick's Vapor Rub will cure everything. This sentiment reminds me of the routine that comedian Chris Rock does, when he says that while he was growing up, cough syrup was the cure-all for every ailment. My aunts and uncles came by, we found my father's military discharge papers, and we took him to the V.A. Hospital, but they wouldn't keep him. We went over to Rush, and that doctor prescribed some Dalmone pills to help him sleep.

On August 11, he was admitted to the V.A. Hospital for the pain. The next day he was using a wheelchair because he said his legs hurt so badly. On the evening of August 13, all of my father's children were at the hospital during the same time. This included all my siblings, and Gloria Jean who flew in from Tennessee. The doctor had earlier told us that the cancer was spreading rapidly and that my father's balance wasn't steady. "Could someone spend the night with me?" my father asked. But the hospital rules dictated that my father wasn't seriously ill. So no one was allowed to stay with him. As I left my father, he wasn't saying too much, he was just looking vulnerable. The next morning,

August 14, I went to work as usual, but I had awakened so early, going up to the attic to try to find my birth certificate. This was weird, since the attic had to be hot during this time of year. Around 10:20 a.m. I received a call from Phyllis. "I think R.D. just died," she said. I felt a loss for words—a father—just empty. As I hung up with Phyllis, Olivia called me. I prepared to leave and told my boss. Phyllis, Olivia and I met up because we all worked in the same vicinity. We took a cab over to the V.A. Hospital and went into my father's room. In a weird way, I recall what I wore to work that morning: a short, electric blue suede skirt, with a gold top and gold, suede shoes with nail heads on them. I remember because when I arrived at the hospital, I felt sort of strange with this near mini skirt on going to pay my respects.

Audrey says she remembers that she was fortunate to have been able to celebrate her birthday with him one last time. She also recalls the last night when we were all at the hospital to see R.D. on that night before he died. "Then I went back to work on Thursday. I worked at Carson, Pirie, Scott & Co. at the time and I was on break," she said. "I was trying to get back to my desk, and the elevators were slow and I was stalled on the first floor for a bit." She recalled that by the time she got back to her desk, she learned that R.D. had died. "He was so popular that his obit was in the *Chicago Sun-Times*."

When we all arrived at the hospital, R.D. was laying there peacefully. The nurse said that my father had gotten up, had breakfast and was sitting in the wheelchair while the nurses were making the bed. He vomited and his head went back. The doctors and support staff tried to revive him but it was too late. They called it cardiac arrest; due to lung cancer. Just like that, at the young age of 60, he was gone.

No more peanut brittle and coconut bars, or Whitman's chocolates for my mother on Valentine's Day, or nice suede Native American-style moccasins just out of the blue. No more waiting while my father popped popcorn on the stove the old-fashioned way. No more surprise gifts like the nice crème knit dress he once bought me or the mesh gold watch that he also gave me as an adult. No more watching my father sit at the kitchen window in his boxers, with his legs crossed, cigarette in hand—just waiting for his sweet potatoes to finish roasting in the oven. No more beans to snap on Saturday mornings. No more Dobbs hats, white pocket hankies or light-colored patent leather shoes. Don't laugh, real men wear patent leather shoes! My father would no longer hold court in his garage, with men spilling out into the driveway, while one or the other either had his car fixed or watched along as someone else's car was being repaired.

The newspaper clipping about his death described him as being from the South Side and as being a "metals company maintenance worker" and acknowledged that he had been employed by the Gary Steel Supply Company for more than seventeen years prior to that.

Randolph Hegwood Sr.

Randolph Hegwood Sr., 60, a metals company maintenance worker, died Thursday at the Veterans Administration Westside Medical Center.

Mr. Hegwood, of the South Side, had been a maintenance worker at Universal Metal Service Co., South Holland, for two years. Previously, he had worked for Gary Steel Supply Co. for more than 17 years.

Survivors include his wife, Pinkie; a son, Randolph Jr.; and five daughters, Audrey, Elaine, Phyllis, Charise and Gloria Jean.

Other obituaries for that day profiled people who were in their 70s, 80s and 90s. My father was much younger and didn't belong on that page—not then. "The church was so crowded, I just knew the mayor of Englewood had died," my girlfriend Belinda later told me. And indeed it was crowded. Relatives had come from out of town; some of them driving in from Michigan on a weekday afternoon for the funeral and driving back home that night, so they could make it to work the next morning. People were lined along the walls and outside on the church steps. The Block Club sent flowers. There was one floral arrangement with the time that my father died—10:15. My sister Phyllis tried to sing *Amazing Grace* but just couldn't make it through the entire song. How could she?

Randolph Hegwood Sr. outlived the richness of our neighborhood. And from 1949 when my parents married until 1986 when my father died, he did what a responsible black man with a family was supposed to do—he took care of us. Now, I am not saying that my father was without faults but NOT taking care of his family and sitting at home waiting on the government dole wasn't one of them.

I was at home once, years after my father died, and a man knocked on the door, inquiring about the man who owned the garage. I sadly told him that my father had passed and he acknowledged as much, saying that he knew that something must have happened.

Twenty

Ms. Pinkie Turns 80 years old

My mother recently turned 80, and family, friends, and former co-workers from near and far helped her celebrate in grand, Gospel style. During a more than four-hour celebration, a local all-female Gospel group provided entertainment, while family and guests showered my mother with love and salutations. Fellow members of her church, which is now called the New Trinity Missionary Baptist Church, were as excited as Ms. Pinkie about the event and her long, God-fearing life.

"She is such a sweet person," said Trinity's first lady Gloria Jenkins, whose husband, Jewel, is Trinity's pastor. "She is a virtuous woman to me and full of the Holy Spirit—she is directed by the Lord." Jenkins added that Ms. Pinkie is an inspiration for all in the church and the community. "She is a light for us in the church, especially the younger women. She has a 'fence ministry' in the neighborhood to all who will listen." Jenkins said that many people don't obey God's instructions but that Ms. Pinkie lets people know what the Lord has for them. "I thank the Lord for her obedience because she always lets us know what the Lord has on her heart for us." Others were also happy to join the festivities: "I have been knowing her since I was in the first grade, and she is just like a mother to me," said Sandra Monegan. "She is my rock and has brought me through many things. When she prays for me she has the anointing on her."

My mother serving as a support system was how many others described her: "I met her in 1985, and we have stayed on the phone a long time when talking about the Lord," said Mary Herron. "She truly loves the Lord." Neighbor Brenda Hawkins said: "She is like a second mom to me and she is really nice and thoughtful." Another long-time friend and former Trinity member had an amusing story about Ms. Pinkie during church services. "Whenever you are singing and it reaches her, she will beat you in the back like nobody's business." For those who may not understand that last quote, my mother isn't beating someone in the back in a harmful way. She is tapping that person on the back, in agreement that the person who is singing is doing a good job of heralding in the "presence of the Lord." That presence was very much evident during my mother's party, as family members paid tribute to Ms. Pinkie for her unyielding hard work in raising a bunch of children who very much appreciated the sacrifices that she made to ensure that we all had the tools that we needed to survive and prosper—even in the midst of what can be seen as the "craziness of our surroundings in Englewood." The party capped off a nearly two-week run of mini festivities, including the gift of my 46-year-old nephew's presence, whose trip to Chicago from Atlanta had my mom just slightly hysterical. Phyllis and her husband also came in from New Jersey. My brother R.L. Barrett, who lives in Shaw, Mississippi, sent his salutations. In the end, my mother basked in all of the love that everyone agreed was surely deserved. And we kids from Englewood were equally as proud.

The Hegwood Family celebrates Ms. Pinkie's 80th birthday.
Ms. Pinkie, Randy (front); Elaine, Audrey, Phyllis, Olivia (back)

Ms. Pinkie's birthday party, circa 1985.
Cristalle Elaine, Olivia (front); Phyllis,
Elaine, Ms. Pinkie, Audrey (back)

Epilogue-Drug Dealers Don't Get Halos

Since I started writing this book and within the last two years a friend of mine, Evangelist LaDonna Price, lost her only two children—two sons—to Chicago's violence. The youngest, Aaron Price Sr., was shot more than a dozen times and died in January 2012 at the age of 32. Her surviving son, Anthony Price Jr. was stabbed to death at the age of 35 during a domestic dispute in August 2013. Both crimes occurred on the North Side of Chicago, in areas that decades ago didn't even count many blacks as residents. And as illustrated in the *Crain's* video series, both funerals were arranged and conducted under the direction of Leak & Sons Funeral Homes.

I covered Aaron's funeral and wrote the following article on January 21, 2012, titled *"Mom, pastor of Chicago man shot 17 times preach hope: CeaseFire's Ameena Matthews also encourages hundreds,"* which appeared in the *Chicago Crusader* and other media outlets—not only in the Chicago area—but across the country.

Those reading news accounts about his shooting death have chimed in on message boards that it's just another black man dead, and that his death helped to "thin out the herd." But for those hundreds of family, friends and mourners who turned out to celebrate Aaron Price Sr.'s life on a recent frigid Tuesday morning, he was not just another fatality. He belonged to a family and had close friends who loved him.

Price was found shot dead January 10, at the age of 32, in an alley in Edgewater on Chicago's North Side. His mother, Evang. LaDonna Price—as hundreds of black mothers across the nation—doesn't want his death to be in vain. She admonished those at his service to wake up and accept Jesus Christ and have faith that there are better ways to live. And judging by the dozens of young people who answered the call, just maybe Aaron's passing might mean more than just another black man making the wrong choices and having his lifestyle catch up with him.

As hundreds of people filed through the South Side church—Aaron's father, Anthony, some older family members and friends, but mostly friends who appeared to be in their 20s; some even wearing garments that celebrated Aaron's gang lifestyle—many probably wondered how such a young man could attract so many people. Everyone agreed: Aaron was the life of the party and would always make you laugh. But Aaron didn't always heed the advice and values his mother tried to stress, while raising him and his brother, who is one year older.

Price shared with the crowd that she ignored an assignment that God gave her many years ago to reach out to the youth and that as a result many lives were lost. "I don't have tears for Aaron right now," she said. "I am grieving for you all." She told stories of looking for her son as he was out in the street dealing drugs and running into many of the people who now mourned his death.

She recounted stories of when Aaron was in jail and he said he would talk about the Bible to other inmates, always promising to do better when he was released. But as many black men have done before him, he just couldn't let the street and fast money attained by drug dealing go. "He was doing everything and anything that he wanted to do, even after I poured all I could into both of my sons to show them the right way to live," Price added.

She spoke of the prodigal son, who in the Bible left home but eventually returned to his father. "However, Aaron never made it back home," she said. "I can't put him in Heaven, because of his lifestyle, and you all have choices," she told the audience. "But his lifestyle hurt and harmed people." As the mourners waited for her next words, many still believing he was the model son, Price jolted some to reality: "You just don't get shot 17 times for nothing." Autopsy reports show that Aaron was shot 17 times, and his hands were covered with gloves in the casket.

His death greatly pains Aaron's father, who loved and will sorely miss him. "I'll never forget the good times we shared, always thinking you should have been spared," was his poem to his late son. "But it's not my call."

However, the funeral didn't appear to be services for a gang member; everything was peaceful and there were no instances of conflict. But this is a fact that Pastor Olivia Johnson (my sister) of Chicago-based Generational Blessings Family Worship Center, of which the Prices are members, wanted to impress to the audience. "You spend so much time on Facebook, putting halos up to remember Aaron," she said. "But he sold drugs to children and he hurt families. Don't let his dying be in vain. Drug dealers don't get halos, and drug dealers don't go to Heaven, not even our sons."

After imploring those to turn from the streets and to go back to school and become productive adults, Pastor Johnson prayed for dozens of youth who joined at the altar, many becoming swept up in the spirit.

To further spread a message of reform and hope, Ameena Matthews shared her story of transformation, after growing up as one of the oldest children of noted Chicago El Rukin gang leader Jeff Fort. "We have lost countless brothers on the street," Matthews, who is enjoying phenomenal acclaim for her starring role in the violence intervention documentary The Interrupters, told everyone. "I went through the same journey and thought I was invincible."

She advised the mourners to take the love they had just experienced by hearing the eulogy saying, "Your promise to the Creator can't be forgotten." She encouraged the older people in the audience to take younger ones under their wings. "We can't keep killing one another, just because we have an argument doesn't mean we have to shoot."

Indeed, Aaron's death is not in vain, says Pastor Johnson. "The service made an immediate impact on the crowd, for within a few days afterward, Facebook postings were no longer filled with profanity and anger but now spoke of simple condolences and fond memories, along with a notice that the Facebook page memorializing Aaron and reflecting his lifestyle would voluntarily be removed by week's end. Also, young people who had been living wayward, destructive lives outside of their family homes were returning back home for guidance."

But here we were again; about 20 months later on August 10, 2013, listening to Evang. Price eulogize her surviving son, Anthony. And although the circumstances of the two deaths are vastly different, the end result was the same—two black men killed during the face of violence within the streets of Chicago. Between the two brothers, there are eleven children left to find their way and to try to make productive lives for themselves. Evang. Price with much dignity said that, "She didn't have any more sons to give up to the violence in Chicago." And again, she encouraged the friends of Anthony to turn from the streets and live a life for God, as well as encouraged the young women at the funeral to not engage in lifestyles that would lead them to have babies out of wedlock. She mentioned that she noticed a difference in the response to her second son's death, saying that the dozens of people who visited her before didn't knock on her door this time. Could it be those people from Aaron's and Anthony's generation are becoming desensitized to violence and that they expect these things to happen to their friends; they expect to lose contemporaries during their lifetimes?

Believe me, I know that Evang. Price isn't the first mother to bury more than one child to street violence. But I don't know those other parents. I know Evang. Price and I know that this is a mother who is hurting. But it is also a mother who loves God and has forgiven those involved in her sons' deaths. With forgiveness as the theme, it is imperative that young blacks in Englewood, across the city, and in other parts of the country—world even—learn conflict resolution skills. Please don't remind me about all the arguments for social programs, jobs, and improved educational opportunities. Even with these things being enhanced, there still has to be a love for people to stop this carnage. There also has to be a respect within the black community for our past. We must recognize and respect the injustices that black men and women have had to overcome—all in the name of equality for us all. This, along with the many other injustices and lives lost to the movement, deserves more respect and acknowledgement than the black community is currently displaying.

Blacks who came to the Northern and Western cities of the nation made a way for themselves and were undeterred when it came to making sure that their families were sheltered, clothed, and fed. There was a respect and concern for the community in ways that had been nurtured down South. Folks cared for the well-being of those around them. If you were living in the tenement and someone didn't have food to eat, then one family would share with the next. In other words, migrants from down South worked hard, but other generations after them somehow missed a step when it came to that. After having lived in Chicago for nearly sixty years, I know that things were so much better decades ago.

Finally, for the thousands of people who call Englewood home, life goes on even in the midst of all the negativity. People still get up to go to work, see their kids off to school, come home from work to cook dinner, and prepare their families for church on Saturday night—just as my parents did more than fifty years ago. I realize that some people from a generation other than mine might find it hard to believe that blacks lived together and worked together for the good of all in the community. They might find it hard to believe that killings and murders were *not* a daily occurrence and certainly weren't carried out just for the sport of it.

For me, however, it is not hard to imagine when young teens could have a good time, either jumping Double Dutch in the neighborhood or at the movies (not worrying about a civil outbreak or fight between gang members). When the Black Panthers were the main gang in town and doing good in the community. When parents stayed together through good and bad, thick and thin, for the sake of the entire family. When even in those households without fathers, the male children obeyed and respected their mothers or aunts or grandmothers. When social programs worked, and children and young teens embraced the idea of learning and making it out of the 'hood. When a young sustah could come home from work at midnight, riding the "EL," not having to worry about someone yanking her life away from her while on that train.

Much has changed, and life goes on, but this, too,—the jungle that some parts of Chicago have become, even earning the city overall the name *Chiraq*—shall pass.

I can conceive of no Negro native to this country who has not by the age of puberty been irreparably scarred by the conditions of his life. The wonder is not that so many are ruined, but that so many survive.

-----*James Baldwin, Notes of a Native Son*

And I can hear Randolph Hegwood Sr., with a smile as wide as the grill on that Red Buick Riviera, saying, "Pankie, you done messed around and let that girl write a book!"

Mom and R.D., circa 1960

Psalm One and Elaine Hegwood Bowen

Cristalle Elaine Bowen and Elaine Hegwood Bowen, circa 1985.